THE PURSUIT OF
SOMETHING
BETTER

THE PURSUIT OF
SOMETHING
BETTER

HOW AN UNDERDOG COMPANY DEFIED THE ODDS, WON CUSTOMERS' HEARTS AND GREW ITS EMPLOYEES INTO BETTER PEOPLE

Dave Esler and Myra Kruger

The Pursuit of Something Better
How an Underdog Company Defied the Odds, Won Customers' Hearts, and Grew
Its Employees into Better People

Published by
New Ridge Books
2717 Ridge Road
Highland Park, IL 60035
United States of America

ISBN   978-0-9824437-0-5
Library of Congress information on file with Publisher

The Pursuit of Something Better/by David Esler and Myra Kruger 1st ed

Printed in the USA
First Printing
Trade Edition

*This book is dedicated to the loving memory
of Jesse Reynolds Esler, who always believed that
words mattered, and that all problems could be solved if things
are said clearly, and with integrity and love.*

CONTENTS

Part III: Defending the Dynamic Organization

Part IV: Taking it to the Streets

IN APPRECIATION

We are lucky. We have lived our dream, but it would not have been possible without the support and love we have had from so many. A few deserve special mention:

First and foremost, **Jack Rooney**, whose complete honesty throughout this process enabled us to do our best and most fulfilling work.

Connie Rogers, our lasting friend and first partner in this search.

Lou Lehr, former CEO of 3M, and **Jean-Pierre Maurer**, former CEO of Metropolitan Life of Canada, who showed us the first glimmers of something better through their people-centric leadership.

Jim Wilkes, former VP of HR, and **Frank Zimmerman**, former president of Illinois Bell, who tested and validated the value of all the elements of our work that came together later at U.S. Cellular.

Jeff Childs, who generously shared his calming wisdom with us when we got discouraged by the detours we encountered.

Catherine MacCoun, who brilliantly lent her skills and kept us disciplined so that this book would be completed while demonstrating incredible patience with our learning.

Karen Wierer, who for the last nine years, has been our right hand support and all around go-to person for the culture survey process and the Leadership Forum, and **Dawn Moore**, who made thousands of meetings and events happen for us.

FOREWORD

I t is one of life's great privileges to work in an environment where an entire organization has embraced a common purpose; that opportunity becomes even more special when it comes with the commitment to achieve that purpose honorably. That is exactly what happened on U.S. Cellular's courageous journey from ordinary to extraordinary.

This is the story of a corporate transformation that encompasses not only what my company became, but how it got there. In telling it, Dave Esler and Myra Kruger have provided a roadmap for CEOs and leadership teams who want to deliver results—financial growth and profitability—within a framework of values and principles that their organizations can be proud of.

Most business leaders understand the importance of aligning corporate culture with business strategy. Few companies have succeeded in achieving this goal, however; one of the saddest clichés of contemporary business is the list of values that live primarily on the lobby walls.

U.S. Cellular's story is very different: our culture—we call it "the Dynamic Organization"—is an integral part of our business strategy. The culture is not a separate entity that has to be brought in line with the business—our culture is our business. It is the essential means to achieve all our ends. Our strategy depends on our values—all our values, all the time. As any leader who has tried to balance culture and strategy knows, that formula may sound simple, but it is very difficult to implement. U.S. Cellular's success in doing so is what makes its story important.

Dave and Myra have captured the essence of the Dynamic Organization and its impact on our business, our customers, and our associates. They show how the culture, in all its complexity, came to life. At the same time, they convey beautifully the emotional underpinnings that reveal its simple power.

Whether you are a CEO, an aspiring leader, or a reader hungry for a feel-good story in these troubled times, this book will renew your faith in the possibility of "something better." It will challenge what you think you know about leadership, about what it takes to produce superior results, and about the capacity of ordinary people to achieve extraordinary things.

—Jeff Childs

INTRODUCTION:
THE SEARCH FOR
SOMETHING BETTER

This book tells two stories. One is about U.S. Cellular, a mid-size wireless telecommunication provider, and Jack Rooney, its CEO. U.S. Cellular has thrived playing underdog in an industry of heavyweights because of Rooney's contrarian commitment to a corporate culture driven by old-fashioned, but rarely actualized values: customer focus, respect, ethics, pride. This story is compelling in its own right, a corporate Seabiscuit parlaying a humble pedigree into against-all-odds success.

The other story is bigger than that. It is the even more unlikely discovery, after (in our case) nearly four decades of looking, that there *is* a better way to achieve great results than the conventional, numbers-first, just-the-results-ma'am school of American business.

Many executives, consultants, and (especially) employees have long suspected that there had to be something better than the traditional model, a way of tapping into the emotional commitment of employees instead of alienating it, an approach that would take seriously the unintended old joke, repeated in too many annual reports to be funny any more, that "people are our most valued asset."

There have been occasional sightings of such an animal, tantalizing in their promise, but these have always remained isolated, easily explained by special circumstances: Herb Kelleher's charisma at Southwest Airlines, for example, or the unique vision and exquisite timing of Starbucks' Howard Schultz. Clearly such miracles are not replicable, and so hardly anyone bothers to try.

For us, the pursuit of this better way is grounded in experience. Each of us had the rare opportunity, early in our careers, to see close up the potential of the unleashed human spirit to transform organizations. Those experiences were both blessing and curse: blessing because now we *knew* the possibilities; curse because, in the decades since, our search for a similar situation began to seem like the nineteenth-century obsession with discovering the Northwest passage. We were convinced it must be out there somewhere, but it proved almost impossible to find.

Meanwhile, we talked to people. We have consulted to corporations and non-profits and government and educators since the 1970s, and in that time, we have surveyed more than a million and a half employees. We have had one-on-one interviews with thousands of leaders. The evidence has always been overwhelming that at some basic level, all of them are looking for the same things from their jobs: respect and dignity; some indication that they are valued as individuals, not just as hired arms or backs or brains; the belief that they are engaged in an ethical pursuit for an ethical organization; and a sense that they are contributing to a purpose higher than enriching their bosses and owners. This has never changed. When employers persist in acting as if the employee relationship were purely an economic negotiation, those core desires go beneath the surface, buried in apathy, cynicism, and rage, but they never disappear.

We found, over the years, many people who agreed with us. Some of them have been corporate executives. Very few of them, however, have ever been in a position to bring those beliefs to fruition. The stars never seemed to be aligned just right—the economy turned bad, a supportive CEO took early retirement, an unexpected merger introduced unsympathetic ownership. Always something. We even had a promising situation evaporate when the prospective change agent dropped dead in his office, at least thirty years too soon. At one point, the only way we could keep this dream alive was to form a group of like-minded believers—leaders from some of the country's most respected companies—that we called the "consortium," a kind of underground cell dedicated to sharing intelligence and shoring up member morale.

We had almost given up by then. No Northwest Passage. No white whale, either. Just more and more dispirited employees telling us how much they hated their jobs and their bosses. Then, nearly fifteen years ago, we met Jack Rooney, and his story and ours intersected, with U.S. Cellular as the place where we all finally got the chance to explore our dreams.

Rooney would be the first to reject the notion that there is anything special about him. He is a humble man, with little of the slick sophistication common to boardrooms (although that in itself qualifies as "special"). U.S. Cellular was a very ordinary company. Its founders and principal owners, Chicago's Carlson family, wanted to build it into a premier wireless communication company, and they were open to Rooney's ideas on accomplishing that mission. Beyond that willingness to look beyond the tried and true, the company had no unusual blessings that defy replication.

That openness to change and wholehearted support by the Carlsons throughout the process has paid off spectacularly. The company's success demonstrates convincingly what we have long known: that there *is* a better way; that bigger, better, and more lasting results can be achieved by overturning some of the most sacred tenets of the conventional business model; that putting people first works best; and that anyone with the will and the heart can do it.

PART 1

The Visionary and His Vision

CHAPTER

SNAPSHOTS:
U.S. CELLULAR NOW AND THEN

SATURDAY, SEPTEMBER 8, 2007, 10:00 A.M.

U.S. Cellular's huge retail store in Lansing, Illinois, a gritty south-side Chicago suburb, is gearing up for one of the critical weekends of the back-to-school selling season. A full roster of twenty sales associates is working the store today, ready for the expected onslaught of several hundred customers, many of whom are already there, checking out the new hand-set lineup, paying bills, picking up accessories. Every new arrival gets the same warm greeting: "Welcome to U.S. Cellular," accompanied by a hand-shake. The store is starting to hum; it is already clear that this is going to be a very good day.

2:00 P.M. THE SAME DAY

The 75 customer service representatives on duty at U.S. Cellular's Tulsa, Oklahoma call center (one of five across the country) are bearing up well under the usual weekend deluge of customer inquiries. Saturdays are always busy, and service levels—the way call centers measure their responsiveness—are often lower than they are during the rest of the week. This is the first weekend after the Labor Day holiday, and call volumes have been even higher than normal.

Still, the center is calm, with only the collective buzz of dozens of simultaneous conversations breaking the quiet of the floor. The mood is intense, purposeful, focused. As one call succeeds another, associates eye the electronic board that provides a running update on how the center is doing in meeting U.S. Cellular's commitment to make customer service its calling card. The news is good so far: service levels are four percentage points higher than expected, and rising. It looks as if the reps are building some momentum to carry over into Sunday, when things figure to be equally busy.

SUNDAY, SEPTEMBER 9, 3 A.M.

All's well at the National Network Operations Center in Schaumburg, Illinois, not far from U.S. Cellular's Chicago headquarters. The usual weekend night crew of a dozen technicians monitors a wall of screens depicting the internal workings of the company's network of thousands of transmission towers and switches, instantly identifying any malfunction that threatens customer service anywhere in the country. Their job is to spot the trouble, identify its cause, and if the problem requires local attention, notify the nearest on-call network engineer.

This has been a quiet night so far—the best kind in a place where no news is good news. The entire weekend, in fact, is uneventful, a tribute to the tip-top condition of a network that has become a point of pride for the whole company.

Sunday afternoon, 3 p.m.

As this gorgeous late-summer weekend draws to a close, the same scene is repeated in U.S. Cellular stores and call centers and engineering locations across the country: in Jefferson City, Missouri, Morgantown, West Virginia, and Broken Arrow, Oklahoma; in Appleton, Wisconsin, Bangor, Maine, and St. Louis; in Knoxville, Tennessee and Yakima, Washington, and South Bend, Indiana, and hundreds more. The rush of afternoon activity is interrupted by a phone call: it's Chicago. Sales and service reps strain to catch what they can of the conversation as they continue with their business. Yes, everything here is fine, business is good, customers are happy. No, there aren't any problems. And then a laugh and perhaps a whoop, as the good news arrives in breathless spurts: We've been recognized as one of the company's best! Won a Dynamic Leader Award! Great results across the company! Another J.D. Power trophy too! A big woo-hoo to everybody! Celebrations to come!

As the news spreads, customers share in the high spirits. Many are curious. Who was that on the phone spreading all these glad tidings?

Only as they hear the collective answer—"That was our manager"—does it begin to dawn on them that there are no managers anywhere in the store. There are no managers in the call centers either—no one at all with supervisory responsibilities. None in the Network Operations Center. None anywhere, in fact, across the coast-to-coast breadth of the company.

For this entire weekend, U.S. Cellular has been a company without leaders. Sales and service and technical associates have defied all conventional wisdom by running the business flawlessly, exceeding sales targets and service standards without supervision.

This counters the standard expectations about today's employees: that they are so unreliable, so dislike their jobs, and are so lacking in ethics, self-discipline or loyalty that they will run amok without constant oversight, if they turn up at all. These U.S. Cellular associates seem to come from some kind of parallel universe, or perhaps a nostalgic dream of how things were in a simpler time. They know what to do, they can be depended on to do it, and they do it so well that they easily live up to the elevated expectations of their customers.

Associates have defied all conventional wisdom by running the business flawlessly— exceeding sales targets and service standards—without supervision.

That leaves two big questions: How did this happen? And where in the world are their managers and supervisors?

NOW: A COMPANY OF LEADERS

Sunday, September 9, 7:30 a.m.

If a busy retail store devoid of management is an unusual sight, and a supervisor-free call center unheard of, the scene in the Grand Ballroom of the O'Hare Hyatt at 7:30 on a Sunday morning is equally unlikely. Nearly 1,500 U.S. Cellular leaders are jammed into a theater-in-the round, in their chairs but in such a state of anticipation, exhilaration, and generally high emotion that they can barely sit still.

This follows a feverish hour in which advance agents from each of the company's markets, call centers, and departments have vied with one another to secure prime viewing areas for their teams. By the time each group is in place—most of them wearing matching shirts designed for the occasion and occasionally breaking into team chants—the vast room feels more like a college football stadium than the site of a business gathering.

At 7:30 sharp, the room comes to order—briefly—until Jack Rooney ascends the circular, slowly-rotating stage, when a deafening roar erupts, punctuated by a heartfelt "We love you, Jack!" Rooney is the CEO who made the company what it is today. During his nearly eight-year tenure, he has transformed U.S. Cellular into that rarest of corporate entities: an organization loved by customers, employees, and shareholders alike.

Last night, at the dinner welcoming the leaders, Rooney reported some good news: U.S. Cellular has extended its grip on the coveted J.D. Power Award for customer satisfaction to five consecutive years in its core north-central operations in Illinois and Wisconsin (the only part of the country where it has enough customers to be eligible).

Now his job is to kick off his company's 2007 Leadership Forum, an annual meeting with a single purpose: to share the results of that year's Culture Survey, the highlight of the year in a company that is truly driven by its values.

The Culture Survey is what has brought these leaders to Chicago and created such a state of excited anticipation.

Rooney bet the company's future on his ability to build a culture so strong, so capable of delivering superior customer satisfaction, so unique in an industry where frustrated, unhappy customers are the norm, that his small, regional carrier would find a profitable niche. A self-sustaining organization that could release every one of its leaders for this weekend's events without missing a beat is the result.

Everyone in the room knows, however, that the job is not yet finished. At last year's meeting, the Culture Survey results were disappointing. Some complacency had set in. A number of projects had gone awry, hurting morale. New leaders were not embracing the culture as quickly or as firmly as their veteran peers. While most companies would have killed for the associate commitment evident in the survey numbers, Rooney was not satisfied, and he had challenged his leaders to put things right. The people in this room had tried their best not to disappoint him. For the past year, they had worked hard to deal with their lists of personal and collective challenges. Had they succeeded?

They were about to find out. Rooney introduces Myra Kruger, years ago dubbed "the culture lady," who is presenting the survey results for the eighth time. Kruger has won the organization's trust with the frankness of her morning-long reports on the state of the culture. If the efforts of the past year have not been good enough, she is sure to let them know.

They get their first hint when Kruger reveals this year's response rate: an incredible 97 percent. Most employee surveys attract little interest; return rates rarely exceed 50 percent, and many companies count themselves lucky to hit the 20 percent mark. U.S. Cellular has routinely exceeded 90 percent in the

Rooney era, but even by these elevated standards, 97 percent is out of sight. A good omen.

The answer comes with the very first set of responses, to the statement: "My overall opinion of U.S. Cellular is positive." Even during last year's downturn, two out of three participants strongly agreed with that proposition. How do you top that?

Easily, as it turns out. Ninety-eight percent of this year's responses are favorable, with a breathtaking 76 percent opting for "agree strongly," the survey's highest approval category. Another 22 percent choose "agree somewhat." Just 2 percent disagree, none of them strongly. The room erupts: the news from the culture front is clearly going to be good.

As the morning goes on, the collective mood approaches euphoria. The results for every

These results are not just good—they are almost unimaginable at a time when many American workers are unhappy in their jobs, angry at corporate executives, indifferent to customers, and disillusioned with their companies.

one of the survey indicators have improved, some by spectacular margins. Ninety-one percent agree that "the changes of the past year are moving the company in the right direction." Even more think that their jobs are "very rewarding." Critical results on empowerment and open communication are much improved. "Confidence in senior leaders" is through the roof, with 93 percent offering their approval. As for the company's signature value—customer focus—participants are nearly unanimous (99 percent) in agreeing that serving customers is their highest priority.

These results are not just good—they are almost unimaginable at a time when many American workers are unhappy in their jobs, angry at corporate executives, indifferent to customers, and disillusioned with their companies. As Kruger works through her report, the improvement shown on item after item in the survey exceeds anything anyone in the room had ever thought possible. Communication, training, tools

Rooney has transformed U.S. Cellular into that rarest of corporate entities: an organization loved by customers, employees, and shareholders alike.

to do the job: all way up. It's the same with every question about leadership. Jobs are highly rewarding, work is fun, respect is entrenched, morale is at an all-time high, and most people think they can reach their personal potential within the company. Even work/life balance, usually one of the survey laggards in a very hard-working company, is much better this year.

The discussion of ethics takes some time. Ethics is one of U.S. Cellular's core values, and these leaders have worked hard to convince the entire organization of its importance. This year's response to "people here behave ethically"—91 percent agree—sets off another round of celebration. The spectacle of 1,500 managers of a fast-growing sales organization in an intensely competitive business wildly cheering their own high ethical standards is only one of many surreal scenes on this Sunday morning.

Kruger points out that something important is happening to participants' perception of ethics. What used to be seen as a requirement to stay within the rules has broadened into the much more expansive injunction to "do the right thing" under any circumstances. Judging from the remarkably short list of ethical concerns generated by the nearly 8,300 survey participants, this standard has become solidly embedded.

By 11:00, the audience is in a state of emotional exhaustion. But Kruger has a big finale for them. The response to the question on pride, another core value, is overwhelming: 97 percent answered affirmatively. The people in this room must be among the happiest, most fulfilled workers in the country. Certainly no one among the wildly cheering crowd would argue.

Kruger's report is more than a cavalcade of numbers. What gives the survey results real emotional heft is the words that accompany them: hundreds of direct quotations, drawn either from the write-in section of the questionnaire or from the notes taken at the focus group interviews in which more than a quarter of the company has participated.

Not all of the quotes are positive. The survey's credibility comes from its reputation for reflecting even the most critical perspectives. Even in this triumphal year, many participants are unhappy about how a new payroll system was rolled out. The call centers remain uneasy about the implementation of a customer privacy policy. A significant part of the sales organization is frustrated with the company's deliberate pace in introducing the latest cool technology. The concerns, however, are mere droplets in a bucket of love—love for the company, for the work, for hundreds of "the best leader I've ever had," for the opportunity to stretch and grow as individuals, for corporate values that match the highest personal standards, for the cultural environment that makes all this possible, and for Rooney himself, a CEO who, in one associate's words, "thinks we're more important than he is."

Heart and Soul

In each of the past four years, the participant comments have revealed a distinct theme that marked that year's accomplishments. Four years ago, that theme was "special," as associates began to realize just how unusual their work experience was at U.S. Cellular, and they used that word repeatedly to describe it. The following year, the word that kept popping off the pages of the survey was "love," marking a major escalation of associate affection for their company and what was happening within it. In 2006, even with the downturn in results, there was an outpouring of "thanks"— to Jack Rooney, to their leaders, to all who had made such a unique work experience possible.

This year, Kruger reports, the theme that unites hundreds of comments from all parts of the organization is "growth." Participants, she says, felt compelled to talk about how much they had grown in their time at U.S. Cellular—not just professionally, but personally. They often reached for unaccustomed words like "heart" and "soul" to convey the depth of their feeling about their own transformation into better parents and spouses and citizens because of what they have learned at work.

"My whole life is better because of this company," writes one. "I operate differently at home and in my marriage." Another says, "Our values become part of your whole life.

They've changed mine dramatically." "I'm changing inside," adds a third, "holding myself accountable for things I should have done before." "My empowerment at work has spread to the rest of my life," reports another. One associate spoke eloquently for most of his peers by asking, "Where else can you be grown into a better person?"

As Kruger speaks, the meaning of this year's heretofore obscure conference theme—"Inside-Outside-In"—finally dawns on the audience. The internal culture, she says, has become so strong, so entrenched, that it is spilling beyond the company to affect customers, families, and communities. The goodwill generated among these external audiences then flows back into the company, as they express their appreciation and support with their patronage.

When the session ends, a buzz of exhilaration replaces the deafening exuberance of the morning. These leaders have met Rooney's challenge of

> *"Where else can you be grown into a better person?"*
> —Culture Survey Participant

a year ago to get the culture back on track, but the suspense is not over yet. They won't get their personal report cards on their leadership performance until the meeting breaks up later that afternoon. These reports are based on the survey responses from their own teams and departments, and the results are critical to their careers. U.S. Cellular holds its leaders accountable not only for what they achieve, but for how they achieve it. This personalized survey data is the main input to this "how" dimension.

Some of the group are spared the apprehension. They were honored during the morning session with Coach Awards, presented to the leaders judged by their teams to be the company's best. On the first Culture Survey in 2000, only nine leaders met the exacting criteria for these awards; by 2006, that number had expanded to 40.

Today, the company saluted 115 award-winners as part of the morning's festivities, the tip of a burgeoning iceberg of home-grown leadership talent that prompted Kruger to compare the company to a "leadership factory," churning out waves of leaders—most in their twenties and thirties—adept at taking on a troubled team or project and quickly turning it into a high-performing showcase.

Later that afternoon, Rooney closes the meeting with two new challenges. He charges his leaders first with "defending what we've won." They must guard against complacency and the danger of giving up any hard-earned cultural ground. He then raises the bar one more time. Twelve of that day's award-winners had achieved

The internal culture has become so strong, so entrenched, that it is spilling beyond the company to affect customers, families, and communities.

perfect scores on their personal leadership reports, an unprecedented number. But why not more? U.S. Cellular promises the "ideal customer experience." Shouldn't front line associates be able to expect an ideal leadership experience? The roar that greets this clearly unreasonable request is at least partly due to the audience's relief that their CEO remains, after eight years in office, as feisty, uncompromising and forward-looking as ever. This journey—exhilarating and exhausting and so deeply rewarding—is not, apparently, going to end any time soon.

THEN: WAITING TO FAIL

Sᴜɴᴅᴀʏ, Sᴇᴘᴛᴇᴍʙᴇʀ 24, 2000, 9:00 ᴀ.ᴍ.

It wasn't always that way. U.S. Cellular had convened its first Leadership Forum at the downtown Chicago Hilton, with 300 leaders nervously attending. They were unsure of what to expect from their new CEO who, in his first ten months, seemed dangerously preoccupied with the corporate culture—an exotic topic that had received no previous executive attention.

There were no elaborate, pre-dawn plots to secure good seats. The Sunday crowd was slow to assemble and demonstrated a marked preference for the rear of the house. A few out-of-towners barely made the session at all, stumbling in late under the influence of their Saturday night encounters with Chicago's notorious downtown Rush Street. Mutual lessons learned: the partygoers were sent home, no longer U.S. Cellular leaders, and the meeting never again strayed from the lesser temptations of the O'Hare hotel strip.

The results of the Culture Survey, conducted for the first time during the summer, were equally inauspicious. By normal corporate standards, there was nothing really wrong with the numbers. Most people, for example, had a favorable opinion of their company, with a creditable 89 percent responding positively to that question. Their views were muted, however. Of that 89 percent, well over half were tentative, selecting the "somewhat positive" category. The same pattern applied to the questions on pride, ethics, rewarding jobs, and confidence in senior leaders: lukewarm, semi-positive responses that most companies would be happy to settle for, but not nearly convincing enough to build a culture on.

Some of the numbers were much weaker than that. Communication, tools, and training had not been the company's strong suits prior to Rooney's arrival, and few participants had positive things to say about them. Morale was low in most parts of the company: barely half the survey participants answered that question favorably.

Few of these mediocre results were a surprise, even though U.S. Cellular liked much of what it had seen from Jack Rooney thus far. He had done something about the notoriously low pay for what he called his "front line" associates—the sales and service people that are customers' first contacts with the company—and even threw in a couple of extra holidays. He introduced a casual dress policy. He was more visible than any executive they had met, visiting parts of the company where no predecessor had ever gone. He believed in open communication, installing programs like "Listen Jack" that invited associates to let him know by e-mail what was on their minds, and "Straight Talk," where executives engaged in no-holds-barred information exchanges with groups of associates. This new Culture Survey, in which every single associate was expected to participate, including many in live focus group discussions was part of that package. He had already doubled the number of front line leaders in the stores and call centers, and he had changed their titles from "supervisor" to "coach," to reflect his view of their core responsibilities. To complete the nomenclature revolution, employees had became "associates."

Most of all, he had set out a vision of what he called a Dynamic Organization: a company that succeeded by creating a culture based on values and behaviors that would build high associate satisfaction and unparalleled customer loyalty. At this point, of course, that was all just talk—although Rooney was an exceptionally convincing talker, and he did have a track record of building similar cultures in his two previous companies. Nevertheless, the prevailing mood on the first culture survey was captured perfectly by this write-in comment: "Sounds great, now let's see what happens."

Some of the participants were worried about moving their little company too far, too fast. "We can't just snap our fingers and get the infrastructure built that it takes to make the Dynamic Organization work," complained one leader." "Go slower, Jack," admonished another.

Beneath the protective layer of caution and "too good to be true" skepticism, however, was an unmistakable core of hope that Rooney had awakened. Before his arrival, U.S. Cellular's

It seemed to most people, however, that the jig was finally up, and that, sooner rather than later, the company would have to surrender to acquisition.

future had been uncertain. It was one of the dozens of small companies that had grown up as an expression of the entrepreneurial spirit of founders who had seen the opportunity in wireless communication but lacked the deep pockets to penetrate much further than the industry's fringes. The company was a hodge-podge of rural and small-town markets scattered to the four corners of the country. It was headquartered in Chicago, where none of its executives or head office associates could buy its services locally.

By 2000, U.S. Cellular had become the eighth largest wireless carrier in the country, but it was dwarfed by industry leaders like Verizon and Cingular (now, once again, AT&T), bankrolled by Baby Bells, or Sprint and T-Mobile, aggressively supported by rich parents. With Wall Street becoming increasingly impatient for the consolidation it felt was long overdue, it was difficult to see a future for a shoestring operation like U.S. Cellular. The company was proud of its resourcefulness in putting together a wireless network with the electronic equivalent of baling wire and chewing gum, and of its success in making good money at it. It seemed to most people, however, that the jig was finally up, and that, sooner rather than later, the company would have to surrender to acquisition. Many associates assumed that Rooney had been hired by the Carlsons, its majority owners, to tidy up the balance sheet in anticipation of the inevitable deal.

"What can we BE, we wonder?"

—2000 CULTURE SURVEY RESPONDENT

Many of the participants in that first Culture Survey expressed those concerns. The uncertainty of their future was one of the top issues to emerge in associate focus groups. Some participants had become so anxious about their situations that they just wanted Rooney to get it over with. Hurry up and sell the company soon, they advised, and put us out of our misery.

And yet . . . . To most people, Rooney did not seem like the kind of leader who was ready to roll over. The changes he had brought so far were aggressive, and he was certainly talking the talk of competition and winning. Maybe, just maybe, he had a plan that would let the company at least survive and find a niche among the industry's big rocks. Anything beyond that was probably too much too ask. This was the minimal hope that Rooney had awakened: that there might be a future for the company after all. One associate dared to express the spirit of optimism beginning to flicker into life by asking this heartfelt write-in question: "What can we BE, we wonder?"

Myra Kruger's presentation to the Hilton audience that first Sunday morning fuelled this hope further. At first the leaders were a wary congregation, hunched as far back as the big room allowed, half expecting to have their various sins pointed out by this new pastor, and uncertain about what kind of expiation might be expected of them. As the morning went on, however, they became increasingly rapt, relieved to have the blunt facts of their work lives out in the open. It became clear that they were not today's targets. Rooney himself said that this first survey was intended only to establish a baseline for the culture change to come. They had nothing to fear, he said—with the pointed proviso that they take the issues seriously and do something about them.

Those issues, for the most part, belonged to the company and its most senior leaders: poor communication, insufficient interest in the needs of either associates or customers, impenetrable department silos, out-of-touch executives. The list went on in breathtaking detail, the survey numbers supported by anonymous participant comments. Questions of ownership aside, everything in the corporate experience of most of the audience told them that someone was going to get fired. Listening to all this reckless honesty carried the same guilty fascination as watching a car wreck about to happen.

It never happened. Rooney, in fact, seemed delighted to be presented with such a daunting list of deficiencies. They came as no surprise to him, he said in his closing remarks, because he had been out in the organization and had seen many of the same problems himself. The relieved leaders poured up to Kruger after the presentation to thank her for describing their situation so frankly. Facing the truth might not save the company, but at least they now had an agenda, a long, long list of personal and organizational shortcomings to address. That was a lot better than, as Kruger had titled one section of her report, "waiting to fail."

Nevertheless, the odds against success were high. U.S. Cellular was in 2000 an organization of just 4,500 people, with a service footprint that made no business sense, a network that needed serious upgrading, and a reputation for tight-fistedness. It made most of its money not from its own customers, but from the "roaming" charges it imposed on other companies when their traveling customers were forced to use U.S. Cellular's far-flung towers. It had no proprietary technology and no discernable competitive advantage. Its employees were neither the best nor the brightest. Many of them were just happy to get a toehold in an exciting, technology-based industry, even if the pay was low and conditions relatively primitive. Few expected to stay with the company any longer than it took to add a credible line to their resumes or work their way through college.

U.S. Cellular's main asset was, in a perverse way, its out-of-the-way locations. As long as the cellular industry enjoyed double-digit growth rates, its competitors had bigger fish to fry in major urban centers. Even that advantage, however, was disappearing, as cellular demand approached saturation and the industry giants began to turn their attention to second- and third-tier markets.

What the company did have was the tiny glimmer of hope generated by Jack Rooney and his magic culture. Very few at U.S. Cellular understood the Dynamic Organization at this point, or believed that it had the power to save their company. But they were David in this battle for survival, there were plenty of Goliaths around, and the Dynamic Organization—feeble though it seemed at the time—was the only weapon in sight.

CHAPTER

2

JACK ROONEY AND
THE DYNAMIC ORGANIZATION

The U.S. Cellular of 2000 seemed to have no future, except as a footnote in some telecom giant's annual report. The U.S. Cellular of 2007 was a roaring financial success, a competitive terror in the growing number of markets where it did business, and the object of an almost cult-like loyalty in its customers and associates. What happened?

The simple answer is that Jack Rooney happened. He brought with him the Dynamic Organization—the D.O. to its friends. The D.O is Rooney's definition of the ideal internal culture for a service organization, an integrated concept of the vision, values, and behaviors that, if fully and consistently implemented, must inevitably produce delighted customers and exceptional results.

By 2000, the idea of culture as a driving force in organizational behavior had just about run its course in most of corporate America. Corporate culture had enjoyed a strong run among the miracle cures and silver bullets of the 1980s and 90s. It had wonderful explanatory power. Why couldn't Detroit build cars of the same quality as the Japanese upstarts who were eating its lunch? Why were some companies (Disney was the example of choice in those days) able to delight their customers consistently, while others drove their patrons to head-banging distraction?

Culture change was a career-killer. It cost a fortune and took forever.

Why were an elite few organizations able to execute their strategies and become business icons? Why did so many of their rivals prove unable to do what they had to do to survive, even when the writing on the wall was in glorious Technicolor? The answer to all those questions was culture. An organization's culture—its values, habits, beliefs and folkways, articulated or not—either enabled it to go in the direction pointed by its planners and strategists or, more likely, formed an immovable barrier that frustrated every well-intended initiative.

For a time it seemed like culture was the key that opened every door. Businesses could get the quality, the productivity, the employee commitment, the sheer excellence they craved simply by aligning their corporate cultures with the desired end. Books, conferences, and consulting careers were all dedicated to the proposition that building a corporate culture was as easy as following a recipe. Just pick the right values from column A to match the right strategy from column B, mix vigorously with cash, and wait for results.

By the mid-nineties, the bloom was off the cultural rose. There were far more failed culture change initiatives than success stories, generating a secondary boom in "What Went Wrong?" articles. Culture change was far more likely to tarnish an executive reputation than advance it. Culture change was a career-killer. It cost a fortune and took forever, as its first champions (Deal and Kennedy, *Corporate Cultures*, 1982) had pointed out. What company had the time and money to spare?

Besides, why bother? By the mid-nineties, there were far more rewarding ways for executives to spend their energies. The surging tide of a booming economy and a rocketing stock market was far more likely to solve business problems than laborious tinkering with corporate values and employee behaviors, and the recent stock option bonanza made a short-term focus on the bottom line far more lucrative as well. Corporate culture became a faded flavor of the month, the fetish of an obsessed few.

Jack Rooney was one of those few. He had become intrigued with the potential of culture to change people and organizations at about the same time that most business leaders were deciding that its career-impeding radioactivity was not worth the time or trouble.

PHILOSOPHICAL ALGEBRA

Rooney is a contrarian among CEOs. He came comparatively late to the role. By the time he got his first corporate operational responsibilities, he was 46 years old. Until then, he had been an observer of CEOs, not a member of the club. Beginning his career as a financial analyst with the Federal Reserve Bank of Chicago, he made his reputation as a problem-solving Treasurer and CFO, a valuable combination of technical acumen and people skills who could be counted on to do the behind-the-scenes heavy lifting involved in a corporate turnaround or an IPO.

In this role, he attracted a range of extraordinary CEO mentors: Charlie Scanlon at the Federal Reserve, Sam Casey at Pullman, John Nevin at Firestone, Bill Weiss at Ameritech. Each was drawn to Rooney, singling him out for a close-up look at what was happening to their organizations, and why. "For whatever reason," Rooney recalls, "I've always been privileged to have a close, unfiltered relationship with the CEOs of my companies. I learned from all of them—what I liked about their approach, what worked, what didn't."

He has little respect for leaders who mask their real beliefs with fine-sounding verbiage, or who lack the courage of their convictions.

By the time he was offered his first operational assignment, at Ameritech in 1992, he was already an unconventional leader: smart, successful, confident, with some firm but untested ideas about what it took to run a business. Typically, he got that job, President of Ameritech Cellular, in a roundabout way. He had left Firestone frustrated. Though he had helped to turn around a company that was in deep trouble, it was sold to a Japanese rival (Bridgestone) before he got the opportunity to "build something." He landed reluctantly at Ameritech, the Chicago-based Baby Bell, as Corporate Treasurer. "I kept saying 'no,'" he recalls, "because I had been there and done that. But Jim Drury [the legendary executive search guru] kept working on me, and after the third interview, I accepted Bill Weiss's promise that if I helped them work through some issues they had, I could move into operations."

Rooney's blunt style was not an easy fit in an executive culture that helped shape his loathing for passive-aggressive behavior. He got difficult things done—streamlined the pension plan, guided the successful IPO of New Zealand Telephone, launched a credit card operation—but his approach infuriated some of his fellow executives.

A potential train wreck was averted when, a year later, Bill Weiss sprang a surprise strategy of "creative destruction" on his too comfortable, too conventional organization. Every executive, and ultimately every leader, had to convince the chairman and his consultants that they belonged in the "transformed" corporation they hoped would emerge. In the carnage that followed, many did not make it, including several of Rooney's nemeses. Rooney himself not only survived, but got the opportunity he had been promised to move into operations. Given a choice of assignments, he picked Ameritech Cellular, one of the smallest of the corporation's ten business units. It was, in the words of the executive who made the offer, " a shitty business," that was somehow managing to lose customers in an industry that was then entering its greatest boom period, growing at a rate of 40 percent a year.

Rooney's own assessment of his new company was that it was in danger of becoming irrelevant. "We were uncompetitive, our associates were demoralized, we gave poor service, and we lied to our customers. Even our executives wouldn't use our phones." Just the kind of challenge he was looking for, and excellent preparation for the situation at U.S. Cellular eight years later.

His long, circuitous route to a corner office was one
reason why Rooney's approach to the job was different than
most of his CEO peers, but it was not the most important.
His upbringing and education had endowed him with a moral
framework that he was unwilling to divorce from his corporate
environment. Categories of right and wrong, he feels, apply to
every human situation, including business. They are no different for the CEO than they are for the front-line associate. Any
conversation with him is never more than a paragraph or two
away from a reference to the "right" or the "fair" or the "ethical" thing to do.

His opinion of unions, for example, while not very high,
is much more nuanced than the knee-jerk antipathy of many
of his executive counterparts. It is shaped by encounters with
unions that were more concerned with maintaining "the union
way" than with doing what was right for their members, yet
tempered by his contempt for business leaders who use their
unions as an "excuse to treat people horribly." In Rooney's mind,
the management vs. union face-off is irrelevant. His focus is
always on his associates. He developed a loathing of executives
who talked the talk about "their people" but failed to put the
words into action. The corporate culture fad just fuelled that
fire. Many companies, he realized, had done an excellent job
of putting the ideal culture on their walls, but almost none of
them had ever tried seriously to implement it. It is the hypocrisy of this contrast that offends Rooney. He has little respect
for leaders who mask their real beliefs with fine-sounding verbiage, or who lack the courage of their convictions.

This moral perspective is not hard to trace. Its source is
about twenty miles, as the crow flies, from his office at U.S.

Cellular's headquarters near O'Hare: Little Flower parish, in the heart of Chicago's old South Side Irish community. A loving family and strong parochial roots formed the core of his outlook, and a Jesuit university solidified it. One of his college courses was "Philosophical Algebra"—as good a description as any of Rooney's own complex mental make-up. An MBA from Loyola University supplied the finishing touch.

"Taking logic and metaphysics taught me how to think," he says. "Reading Plato, for instance, helped me realize that people always act for the good, as they see it. So in business, I always try to give people a noble goal, not just appeal to their selfishness. They will strive hard for something noble, especially if you reinforce their efforts with recognition."

> *"People always act for the good, as they see it. So in business, I always try to give people a noble goal, not just appeal to their selfishness."*
> —JACK ROONEY

The ultimate test of moral grounding in today's corporations is executive compensation. CEO pay, in particular, has become such a wonderland that it has become almost impossible to discuss the topic in terms of right or wrong. It is what it is, and what can you do except take the money and run? Otherwise admired business leaders get obscenely rich in a rigged game and refuse to apologize for it. Jack Welch, for example, was criticized mainly for the tawdry way in which his outsized (and secret) retirement package came to light through an embarrassing divorce, not for the size of the booty (so to speak). Instead of being discredited, he remains an authority on all things corporate.

Rooney is not poorly paid for his services, but he has never negotiated his compensation package. Two days after he had picked Ameritech Cellular as his next assignment, Ameritech Chairman Bill Weiss called, wondering when he was going to ask about his pay. Rooney replied that he wasn't worried: "You'll pay me what the job's worth." He has carried that approach through all of his subsequent positions, creating vast amounts of shareholder value in each and relying in turn on their willingness to meet his own standard of "doing the right thing."

THE VIRTUAL ORGANIZATION

As Rooney assumed responsibility for Ameritech Cellular in 1992, most of the elements of his leadership philosophy were in place, although they had not yet taken shape as the Dynamic Organization.

Rooney concluded that the main influence on how front line associates treated customers was the way their leaders treated them.

One recent experience had been particularly influential. At Firestone, he had been heavily involved in a Bain & Company project that sought to link retail store systems with customer satisfaction and loyalty. The work resulted in an article in the Harvard Business Review and some recognition for Rooney, but its main impact was to convince him that the most critical factor in a retail organization was the interaction between the customer and the front line associate. More important, he came to the conclusion that the main influence on how front line associates treated customers was the way their leaders treated them.

One of the byproducts of the Bain project was an opportunity for Rooney to appear on a panel with CEOs of companies with similar philosophies: Northwestern Mutual, Enterprise Rent-A-Car, Nordstrom. As they told their stories—all variations on the theme that they can get better results by working through people than they could get by running over them—Rooney says that he felt "at home" as an executive for the first time. The apparent effectiveness of this approach just confirmed his instinctive embrace of its rightness. It allowed a leader to "go home at night with a clear conscience."

The final factor in the formation of his thinking was the dislocation caused by the persistent recession of the early 1990s—the "it's the economy, stupid" event that proved the undoing of the elder George Bush. As businesses struggled to shake off its impact, they began to challenge the semi-sacred "social compact" that had characterized labor relationships for decades: lifetime employment in exchange for worker loyalty. It became fashionable to justify lay-offs and downsizing as part of an epic recasting of an obsolete bargain. In its most extreme form, some employers argued that their employees should have to "earn their way in from the parking lot" each day, eternally proving their worth in a nightmarish riff on "What have you done for me lately?" While most companies were unwilling to go quite that far, there was a broad consensus that the days of employment-for-life were over.

At Ameritech—less than a decade removed from Ma Bell, the smothering matriarch of all corporate cultures—many executives found it hard to imagine a working relationship without some kind of underlying understanding. If the old social compact was dead, something would have to replace it. What would the new one look like? Some imaginative suggestions were in the air: steady (not lifetime) employment for employees capable of continuous personal growth, for example, or fair market compensation for value-adding performance. In this heady environment full of new possibilities, corporate walls became festooned with an impressive assortment of proposed missions, visions, and values—the kind of talk without action that raises Rooney's hackles. As he took his position at Ameritech Cellular, he vowed that when *he* decided on a cultural direction for his group, it would happen.

Rooney knew at this point that he was committed to culture change, but his ideas had yet to take coherent, persuasive form. He needed to put all the pieces together, and to do it in a way that he could communicate simply and directly. It was then that he met Myra Kruger.

Kruger and her partner Dave Esler (the authors of this book) had been working with Ameritech's component companies since 1986, dealing with a variety of cultural issues, but trying mainly to help the organization answer the nagging questions that had plagued it since the AT&T break-up and the birth of the Baby Bells two years earlier: Now that we're no longer a monopoly, why don't we feel more entrepreneurial? Why do we respond so sluggishly to competition? *What's the matter with us?*

The answer, of course, was in the culture. Some parts of the organization—notably Illinois Bell—had done an effective job of identifying and addressing some of their underlying cultural impediments. In the course of their work with these units, Kruger and Esler had developed a survey instrument that generated a great deal of revealing data. They were acquiring a reputation as consultants who could help take some of the "mushiness" out of culture.

This was exactly what Rooney was looking for. He and Kruger set out to codify what Rooney had come to believe about people and organizations. The result was the first iteration of the cultural ideal that eventually came to be known as the Dynamic Organization.

At first, Rooney called his ideal culture "the Virtual Organization." He had been reading about the new concept of virtuality: the idea that not all work had to be done in a traditional office setting. The main obstacle to the virtual office was a serious concern about discipline and accountability. If you took workers away from formal organizational structures, would they still give an honest day's work? Rooney thought that they would, if the company's goals and values and behaviors were so thoroughly ingrained that they became reflexive. In other words, a strong culture that was closely aligned with the company's business strategy could produce employees who did not need to be closely supervised and controlled. They would be driven by their own passion and sense of common purpose to achieve at extraordinary levels.

A strong culture that was closely aligned with the company's business strategy could produce employees who did not need to be closely supervised and controlled.

The preamble to the Virtual Organization document sets this goal out in specific terms:

[This company] will be an organization that understands its vision, goals, and standards so well that its values are obvious, and its behaviors are automatically an outcome of the beliefs that have been instilled.

The prospective benefits of such a culture, especially in a retail company with a widely dispersed employee base, intrigued Rooney. "I just thought how neat that would be," he recalls. "In a traditional organization, I would be involved in everything. It would be impossible and exhausting, and I would just muck things up." The Virtual Organization—if he could pull it off—would allow him to focus on providing leadership, while employees ran the business.

The Virtual Organization would not last long as a descriptor of Rooney's culture. The term "virtual" became, during the late 1990s, increasingly associated with outsourcing, with nominally American companies becoming administrative shells for low-wage contractors. That concept is anathema to Rooney. He has consistently resisted, for example, the conventional industry wisdom of shipping call centers overseas. So "virtual" had to go, replaced for several years by the inoffensive but uninspiring "the Desired Culture." By the time he moved to U.S. Cellular in late 1999, however, the old V.O had become the D.O.—the Dynamic Organization.

BETA-TESTING THE D.O.

At Ameritech Cellular, Rooney built a "Kitchen Cabinet" of young leaders who turned the struggling organization around, following his blueprint to the letter. Customers were amazed to have their calls answered by service reps who not only knew what they were doing, but actually enjoyed their jobs. As word of these good experiences spread through the Midwest, prospective employees clamored to get in the doors, and call centers filled with college graduates. Business boomed.

At that point (1995), Ameritech Cellular won the first of five consecutive J.D. Power Awards for customer satisfaction. The company's churn rate (the percentage of customers who leave for other carriers) fell to less than 1 percent—unprecedented in the industry—and stayed there. New customers wanted to join the party. Employee attitudes kept pace with the company's generous contribution to Ameritech's bottom line. Rooney began to attract attention.

Not all of it was positive. Some of his executive peers in other Ameritech units were skeptical of his success, and particularly of its links to culture. The quiet word in the corporate corridors was that anyone could have turned the cellular operation in that kind of hothouse environment. Making money in that business was easy, especially since it wasn't encumbered by the disadvantages of many of Ameritech's other companies: unionized workforces, tired old buildings, unglamorous businesses. Let them run Cellular and stop wasting money on cultural frills and you would see some real profits. The whispers went that it must have been Rooney's Irish luck, more than good management, that had made him a success.

Rooney had his own questions about the juggernaut he had created. He had done what he set out to do, but there was no doubt that the conditions were auspicious. Would the formula work in more challenging circumstances?

He soon got a chance to find out. The largest of the Ameritech operations, Ameritech Consumer Services, was in trouble. This was the regulated land-line telephone company, the heart of old Ma Bell, steward of a declining business at the dawn of the wireless age but stubbornly impervious to change. It was the home of the "Bell-heads," the long-tenured dinosaurs who were judged too set in their ways to be able to function in more entrepreneurial environments. And did we mention that that much of the work force was unionized?

Dick Notebaert (later the CEO of Qwest) had replaced the retired Bill Weiss as Ameritech's chairman, and he had already approached Rooney once, in 1996, about taking charge of Consumer Services. Rooney, who wanted the full five years he had been promised to build the Cellular operation, turned him down. The next year Notebaert tried again. "He handled it the right way," Rooney remembers. "He didn't try to make me an offer or negotiate around. He just asked me to do it. He respected what we had done at Cellular, and he wanted the same things to happen at Consumer, if that was possible." Rooney made the move early in 1997, bringing with him the same cultural apparatus that had worked so well under Cellular's favorable conditions. This, however, would be a far more difficult test.

The next two years were extraordinary, even by Rooney's standards. There was no time, with the Baby Bells competing furiously for supremacy (and probably survival) in an industry long overdue for consolidation, for a leisurely five-year turnaround. Consumer Services may, in fact, have experienced one of the fastest, most tumultuous corporate culture changes in history.

The company had inherited the oldest inner-city facilities of the Ameritech empire, in some of America's dowdiest Rust Belt capitals: Detroit, Indianapolis, Cleveland, Milwaukee, Chicago. Rooney was appalled at the conditions. Even the pay phones in many of his locations were out of order. He embarked on an immediate face-lift, establishing a million-dollar pot for associates in each building to allocate as they chose to improve their physical environments.

Many associates loved Rooney for the impossible changes he wrought in a few months. Some hated him, for the same reason.

A flurry of changes followed, the most significant of which was the requirement that the call center-based customer service representatives conclude every call with a sales pitch for Ameritech's products. Cellular's bright, young work force had leaped at a similar opportunity to broaden the scope of their jobs (and make extra money in commissions), but for Consumer Services' tradition-minded employees, service was virtually a sacred calling, not to be tainted with something as dubious as selling. Rooney persisted, at the same time as he pushed for transformation in leadership, in internal communications, and in relations with the unions. Many associates loved him for the impossible changes he wrought in a few months. Some hated him, for the same reason. A significant number did both.

Kruger recalls the focus groups she and Dave Esler conducted for Consumer Services' Culture Surveys as unlike any she has ever held. "It had been a long time since anyone had asked these associates what they thought about anything," she says, "and Jack had given them an awful lot to think about. We would invite 15 people to a meeting and 25 would show up, whooping and yelling, mad as hell in one breath, thanking their lucky stars that they had lived to see what was happening to them in the next."

If Rooney had any doubts about the power of the Dynamic Organization, the Consumer Services experience extinguished them. A shrinking business when he took it over in 1997, by the summer of 1999 it had become a dynamo, achieving a compounded growth rate of 9 percent—the equivalent of creating a $550 million business every year. The fraternal grousing about Rooney and his culture had abated under the Ameritech roof; several other units had by then adopted various features of the D.O., and Rooney's imprimatur had become a political asset in corporate councils.

This second successful implementation of the D.O. came to an abrupt end when Ameritech became the second Baby Bell to blink in the consolidation wars, acquiescing to expansion-minded SBC's offer. (SBC, seemingly bent on recreating the monolithic Ma Bell from which it had sprung, finally succeeded in turning itself back into AT&T in 2006.) The Texas-based giant was not a hospitable environment for the Dynamic Organization. Even though Ameritech's main attraction was the revenue-generating power of its core Consumer Services and Cellular units, the new owners were not particularly interested in how those big numbers were happening. They wanted Rooney as an operating manager, but not his culture-building paraphernalia. "Culture is for wimps," allowed one member of the take-no-prisoners transition team.

Rooney decided to leave, well-compensated for his efforts, but with a strong sense of unfinished business. He had applied his ideas to build two powerhouse companies, but in each case, he had left before the job was done. He still did not know the full potential of the Dynamic Organization to get results, and, in his mid-fifties, he was running out of time.

ANATOMY OF
THE DYNAMIC ORGANIZATION

Jack Rooney signed on as President and CEO of U.S. Cellular in November 1999, just three months after his departure from Ameritech/SBC. Ted Carlson, the chairman of U.S. Cellular's board of directors, son of the company's founder, knew what he was getting. "We weren't moving fast enough," he recalls. "Competition was heating up, and we didn't seem to have enough forward momentum. Jack was, in many ways, a revolutionary, and that's what we needed."

That's what he got. Rooney could hardly wait to get started. With two successful culture changes behind him—a claim that no more than a very small handful of executives could make—he was confident that he had a winning formula in the Dynamic Organization. Even more important, he had mastered that rarest of corporate tools: a proven approach to implementing fundamental behavioral change.

THE MANIFESTO AND THE BUSINESS MODEL

The vision of the Dynamic Organization that Rooney and Kruger had first developed at Ameritech, and now imported to U.S. Cellular consisted of four parts:

1 **The Preamble**, setting out the vision of a values-driven organization where the behaviors of every associate reflexively follow from those core beliefs.

2 **Seven Key Components:** brief descriptions of what the company will be like for its leaders and associates and customers when the culture is fully in place. These idealized descriptions are the standard against which workplace realities are measured.

3 **Five Core Values:** customer focus, respect for associates, empowerment, ethics, and pride. A sixth Core Value, diversity, was added in 2005. These represent bedrock, ultimate principles against which any action, any proposal, any decision can be tested. None can be bent or compromised.

4 **Ten Desired Behaviors:** the behavioral qualities that Rooney expects to emerge in a company that is truly guided by the core values.

Rooney knew that there was nothing particularly original in this formulation. As newcomers to the Dynamic Organization have been pointing out for 15 years, it represents the ideals that generations of parents, teachers, and clergy have tried to inculcate in their young charges. These ideals could be found by the thousands, nicely framed, in the boardrooms of America, tributes for the most part to some combination of wishful thinking, hyper-active consultants, and corporate cynicism.

What was new was their vital connection to strategy. These values and behaviors were not the classic "nice to haves"—the cultural amenities, the optional extras, that, if one had the time and the inclination, helped make the workplace more pleasant and fulfilling than it would be otherwise. It was this wistful, hypothetical quality ("Wouldn't it be great if . . .") that was starting to give culture a bad name. While there was nothing wrong with trust and openness and respect, they seemed disconnected from—and much too "soft" for—a world that was more comfortable with a "whatever it takes to make the numbers" mentality.

For Rooney, the culture was the strategy. His values and behaviors were not add-ons, interesting things to try if there was time after the real work was done. They were the very essence of how he had succeeded at Ameritech and planned to succeed at U.S. Cellular.

The business model illustrated in figure 1 (*see page 50*) would be his vehicle for converting culture into business results, for translating the intangible language of values and beliefs and behaviors into the hard currency of measurables. It starts with effective leadership, defined according to the Dynamic Organization's Key Components. Leaders model the culture and inspire their people, freeing them from workplace distractions so that they can focus, relentlessly, on their essential role of gaining, retaining, and serving customers and creating the "ideal customer experience." This kind of leadership builds a work environment that is rewarding, stimulating, and fun,

ANATOMY OF THE
DYNAMIC ORGANIZATION

Preamble

U.S. Cellular will be an organization that understands its vision, goals, and standards so well that its values are obvious, and its behaviors are automatically an outcome of the beliefs that have been instilled.

The 7 Key Components

- Associates relentlessly and zealously direct their efforts to gaining, retaining, and serving customers.

- Associates operate close to their customers and are free from the distractions of running the business. The support systems required to serve customers are provided for them.

- Leaders passionately display and continuously promote the vision, values, standards of conduct, and achievements of a winning organization.

- Leaders lead through inspiration, not by regulation, and ensure that other leaders do likewise.

- The organization provides a challenging, learning, rewarding experience for those who work in it; it is fun working here.

- The organization is goal driven, not task oriented. The customer's experience with the

company is more important than the product
provided.

- Associates—especially leaders—have a
customer's perspective and the ability to
visualize the ideal customer experience.

The 6 Core Values

- customer focus
- respect for associates
- empowerment
- ethics
- pride
- diversity

The 10 Desired Behaviors

- common purpose
- passion about the company and our jobs
- trust
- willingness to learn
- openness
- motivation by values, not fear
- enthusiasm
- unselfishness
- flexibility
- confidence in the company, its owner and each
other.

FIGURE 1

resulting in high levels of associate satisfaction. Associates in turn, as the Bain study had proved at Firestone, treat their customers the same way as their leaders are treating them. The result is an extraordinary level of customer satisfaction that builds close relationships and long-term loyalty.

Like the D.O. itself, this business model seems on the surface to be a simple expression of Midwestern common sense. Who doesn't want happy associates and loyal customers? But it was surprisingly revolutionary, representing a direct challenge to the prevailing practices of a wireless industry that was just entering a decade-long binge of wild, sky's-the-limit growth. Customer satisfaction seemed at that time to be an almost irrelevant concept. Why worry about the dissatisfied customers leaving through the back door—even if there were a lot of them—when there were vast hordes lined up at the front? The smart money went into marketing, making sure that your company got its share of all those clamoring newbies, even though you knew that your half-baked network and bored sales people and untrained service reps would soon drive many of them away in teeth-grinding frustration.

Rooney found it incomprehensible that any company would willingly "fire its customers," as he colorfully described the process for an industry publication. U.S. Cellular would do things differently, focusing on the customers it already had, fighting to keep every one of them, building a reputation for outstanding service, and trusting the consuming public to choose that over low price or glitzy marketing.

With business strategy and culture so intimately linked, there was nothing optional about Rooney's Dynamic Organization, and nothing soft about it either. The words he used to describe his ideal culture are not genteel. The vocabulary is strong, tough-minded, even extreme, starting with "dynamic"

> *"Why would any company want to fire its customers?"*
>
> —JACK ROONEY

itself. Associates don't just try hard to please customers, they are "relentless" and "zealous" about it. It is not enough for leaders to be competent and effective; they must be "passionate" and "inspiring." The customer experience is not merely satisfying— it must be "ideal." This is not a culture for the faint-hearted.

"IT SHALL BE DONE."

Rooney builds the Dynamic Organization using four basic tools: an employee survey, internal communications, leadership development programs, and a leadership talent review process. Each of these tools can, in one form or another, be found in almost any major corporation. Rooney makes them uniquely powerful change instruments, however, by shaping them to his own vision and personality. What in most companies are mundane and ineffective programs become, as a result, life-altering (and culture changing) forces.

Granular Evaluation

The Culture Survey is the most striking example of how different Rooney's approach is from corporate convention. Most companies conduct some kind of employee survey, but very few of these focus on the corporate culture, and hardly any in such insistent, obsessive, relentless, and "granular" (Rooney's word) detail. The survey is designed to assess how well the organization as a whole and each individual leader (anyone who supervises at least three associates) reflects the Values and Behaviors of the Dynamic Organization.

That assessment is the collective work of the entire company. While participation is voluntary, every associate is expected to complete the six-page survey questionnaire, which is administered annually. Participation rates are phenomenally high, never dropping below 91 percent and reaching as high as that incredible 97 percent mark in 2007.

Survey response rates are mainly a function of the perceived usefulness of the study. Few companies seem genuinely curious about the opinions of their employees. They conduct surveys mainly because it is expected of them as part of a progressive employee relations posture, or because it is a requirement for some corporate award that they covet. There is little real interest in the data (unless it is highly complimentary), and employees have learned not to expect much action as a result of their participation. The dusty binder of survey data sitting untouched on the credenza of the Human Resources executive is a sad cliché of the survey business.

Not so with Rooney. He has a singular appetite for information about the culture at the core of his business model, and a legendary capacity for acting on it. He has established a personal rhythm around the annual survey cycle, and he expects all his leaders to follow that beat. The Culture Survey identifies critical issues and problems that are inconsistent with the D.O.'s ideals. Leaders study the data, determine what needs to change to address the issues, and take action to implement the fix. The next iteration of the survey measures the effectiveness of their response. Assess, absorb, address, and reassess, over and over.

This is not a culture for the faint-hearted.

Sometimes Rooney's personal rhythm outpaces the annual survey cycle. Associates—especially those who work within the sound of his voice—report that he is happiest when he has fresh data to devour. He gets "grumpy," they say (in tones that suggest a heavy use of euphemism) in those twilight months before the next survey, when last year's issues have been resolved and next year's inevitable fix-it projects have yet to be identified.

In Rooney's view, the survey will always identify problems that require attention. That is what it is intended to do. Some of his leaders, over the years, have been uneasy about what they see as the survey's propensity for focusing on what's wrong with the company, instead of what's right. Rooney's position has always been that he does not need to conduct research to find out what the organization is doing well. Good news practically broadcasts itself. The information he values is about the underground problems, the hidden booby-traps that have the potential to fell a company that allows itself to be taken by surprise.

Still, while he expects the survey to bring these problems to light, it is his unwritten rule that these should be different problems than those of the previous year. Written or not, that is exactly what has happened: every issue raised through the survey process since 2000 has been taken off the table. In a few cases, when the issue was particularly deep-rooted—recruiting D.O.-ready leaders, for example, or addressing the company's perennial data management woes—developing a solution has taken longer than a year. In a handful of others, an especially persistent problem—burgeoning bureaucracy comes to mind—refuses to stay solved, returning to plague the organization after a hiatus of a year or two. But it is to the eternal credit of Rooney and his team that every issue raised anywhere in the company gets a hearing, and every hearing results in an action plan.

It is an unwritten rule that this year's problems should be different from last year's.

Under this regime, U.S. Cellular has understandably developed a self-image of relentless problem-solving. Each year, many write-in comments describe how much associates appreciate the company's willingness to take on the most daunting issues and not let them go until they have been wrestled to the ground. By 2004, associates had started to think of their company as "the little engine that could." More important still, they had developed a level of trust in their company's leadership that is extraordinarily rare.

In this environment, when the company asks associates for

their opinions, who is going to refuse? Virtually every associate appreciates the opportunity to give his/her views, knowing that they will be taken seriously. Survey participation becomes an expectation of the job, a serious part of the responsibilities of an empowered associate, a duty that veteran associates are quick to explain to newcomers.

Another of the survey's key features brings the importance of near-universal participation closer to home. Besides evaluating the broad cultural environment, participants are also asked to provide specific feedback about the leadership of their immediate supervisors. Leadership expectations are clearly defined in the Dynamic Organization, and it is Rooney's conviction that on this critical topic, only the led get to vote. A 29-item battery of questions asks them to assess their leaders on all the key behavioral dimensions of the D.O. Their responses form the basis of the score assigned to any leader with three or more reports. This score is an important factor in judging leadership performance. Through their participation, associates can thus shape the quality of the leadership they receive.

Nothing is more characteristic of Rooney than his decision several years ago to expand this leadership component of the survey to include not only the immediate supervisor, but the leader at the next higher level. He had become suspicious that some leaders were manipulating the "three or more direct reports" rule to ensure that they would not receive a survey score and thus operate under Rooney's radar. If any leaders tried to hide in this way, the expanded survey would flush them out from two reporting levels away.

The written questionnaire is the core component of the

Culture Survey, but even more important—and certainly more unusual—is the extensive network of interviews conducted at the same time. More than a quarter of the company's associates (now approaching 9,000) take part in 90-minute interviews, most of them in groups of ten to twenty, answering questions about their day-to-day experience of the Values and Behaviors.

Their comments are used to interpret the data from the written questionnaire and to answer the questions posed by the survey numbers. What was behind the surge in pride in the New England market? Why did morale tank in Washington? What's causing the loss of confidence in senior leaders among store managers? Who lit a fire under the Knoxville call center? Interview participants, assured of confidentiality and confident that their views will be taken seriously, are happy to offer their opinions on such questions.

Much of the impetus for the interview process comes from Rooney. In the first years of the Culture Survey, his insatiable curiosity about why the results were what they were led us to begin probing participants through these discussions. At first, we interviewed a relatively small sample of the organization. In 2000, for example, we conducted interviews in seven of the 20 markets that U.S. Cellular then served. Rooney's quest for granularity, his zeal to know every soft spot and vulnerability in the organization, drove us to increase the number of locations each year, until by 2003, the mandate was to "go everywhere."

The same impulse to expand constantly the amount of cultural information before the organization is threatening to turn the Culture Survey into a year-round process. Rooney has been tinkering with a "mid-year" survey since his Ameritech Cellular days, either as a spot-check to keep the organization on its toes, as a method of providing additional course-correction data for troubled locations or departments, or as a way for curious leaders to get advance feedback prior to the main survey on changes they have initiated. Even after the stellar results of the 2007 survey, there were enough of these "units of interest" for Rooney and Jay Ellison, his Chief Operating Officer, to commission nearly a dozen such studies.

> *On the topic of leadership, only the led get a vote.*

The Infrastructure of Open Communication

Employee communication, ignored and undervalued almost everywhere else, plays a critical role in Rooney's program. In his view, culture change takes place along a continuum that starts with awareness (of the need for change and what that change will look like), then builds understanding (which may or may not also include agreement), moves toward acceptance as participants realize that the change could very well be good for both company and individual, and ultimately extends to full engagement and commitment. Instrumental in reaching each of those stages is the purposeful use of a strategic internal communications program.

At the start of this process, when awareness and understanding are the goals, an intense focus on the new message is essential. The only information worthy of the organization's attention at this point is that which advances the Dynamic Organization. Everything else is a distraction. When Rooney came to U.S. Cellular, there was a tremendous amount of communication activity. Every call center and region and many departments had their own newsletters, all of them focused on "news" featuring the activities (mostly extracurricular) of employees, but little real communication about the essentials of the business. He abolished them all, replacing them with a single vehicle for the whole company, called **Dynamically Speaking**.

Rooney has always insisted that employees have a right to know why.

That publication focuses solely on the culture, and the events and achievements that advance it. Its mission was (and still is) to redefine what was important to the company and its people. Gone were the employee birthdays and bowling scores, replaced by examples of the D.O. in action: associates demonstrating above-and-beyond customer focus; leaders applying enlightened associate empowerment to solve thorny customer issues; teams unified and mobilized by the power of pride.

Dynamically Speaking is also one of the key forums where the most important question of culture change can be asked and answered: Why? The change environment is fast-moving, with leaders making dozens of decisions to reshape the organization and redirect its agendas. These decisions can easily appear to associates to be random "noise," part of a confusing maelstrom that makes them feel like passive victims of change instead of participants. In *Dynamically Speaking*, the company's actions are explained, their rationale carefully laid open and connected to the larger goals they are intended to promote.

Rooney has always insisted that associates have a right to these explanations, a right that is exercised through the liberal use of the question "why?" Early in his U.S. Cellular tenure he was having trouble getting his leadership team to grasp the appropriateness, let alone the necessity, of having associates question their decisions. He underlined his point by distributing to every leader big buttons, to be worn at all times during office hours, emblazoned with the message, "ASK ME WHY." Besieged by curious associates, they soon understood that "providing the whys" was a vital part of their leadership roles.

Associates reacted to *Dynamically Speaking* with an enthusiasm rarely accorded internal publications. Unlike its predecessors, it contained vital information that could reveal the mysteries of this new world they were entering and show them what they needed to do to find a place in their changing company.

Rooney brought with him to U.S. Cellular a number of other communication institutions that had proven their practical and symbolic value in the implementation of the D.O. One was the Culture Survey itself, which is as much a communication device as it is a research instrument. By repeatedly asking everyone in the company the same questions about leadership and company behavior, and by attaching such life-and-death importance to the results, the survey makes it clear to everyone what is truly important to the organization and what is not.

Rooney underlines those points by making the annual **Leadership Forum**, devoted exclusively to the presentation of the survey results, the focal point of each leader's year. This is the one time that the company's entire leadership team gets together, and the only item on the agenda is the culture. New leaders recruited from other companies who experience this for the first time shake their heads in amazement at the seriousness with which U.S. Cellular treats this material, but they get the unmistakable message. By the time they have experienced their first Forum, they have often moved through the entire awareness-understanding-acceptance-commitment continuum on a single emotion-filled weekend.

Another of Rooney's tried-and-true communication devices is **Listen Jack**, an invitation to anyone in the company to e-mail him personally to say anything they want to say: a general gripe, a specific complaint, an idea, a thank-you, or just an observation. Every item is guaranteed a response, either from Jack or the executive accountable for that issue. Rooney monitors all of the correspondence. This e-mailbox generates up to a thousand messages a year, and inspired a spate of departmental and local imitators. Collectively, these programs underscore the value the company places on truly open communication. As one associate wrote on the culture survey, "You never have to accept a No here that should be a Yes."

Probably none of Rooney's innovations prompted more leadership heartburn than Listen Jack. In a company where the sanctity of the chain of command was probably the one leadership principle on which everyone agreed, Listen Jack seemed to many to be a recipe for anarchy, with associates invited to go over their leaders' heads to tattle to a sympathetic new CEO, who seemed disturbingly eager to find excuses to rattle cages and disrupt the accepted ways of doing things. Several leaders, accustomed to working in an organization where geographical distance and lack of executive interest had given them license to run their shops their way, made it clear to their people that Listen Jack was off-limits. Some of their associates, however, were emboldened by the new regime to report instances of local repression, using either the Culture Survey or Listen Jack itself. After investigation confirmed their stories, the offending leaders were terminated. Rooney e-mailed everyone in the company to report what had happened and why: an eye-opening lesson on the deadly seriousness with which crimes against the culture were now being handled.

Another key communication initiative is the **Straight Talk** program that puts senior executives in front of groups of associates several times a year for a freewheeling exchange. These leaders bring with them detailed explanations about the company's latest plans and initiatives and decisions, and

"You never have to accept a No here that should be a Yes."

associates bring their ideas, concerns, and questions. This vehicle formalized U.S. Cellular's transition from an organization where executives were only a rumor to one in which senior leaders are known to nearly everyone by their first names and trusted like family.

One of Rooney's most compelling traits is his own openness to new ideas; he will make instant adjustments to his successful formula as soon as the data suggests the need. When the 2006 survey data indicated that directors—a key leadership level—were showing signs of skepticism about the company's direction, he immediately started a Directors' Forum, a quarterly meeting dedicated to giving them greater access to the company's strategic planning processes. By the next year, all signs of the problem had disappeared, and the new Forum had become an instant institution.

The last piece in Rooney's communication puzzle is the annual **Kick-Off Meeting**, a first-quarter road show extravaganza that combines a celebration of the past year's achieve-

THE COMMUNICATION INFRASTRUCTURE

Dynamically Speaking

Company newsletter focused exclusively on what's happening in the culture and why.

Listen Jack

Anyone in the company can email the CEO with questions, comments or complaints, and get a prompt reply.

Leadership Forum

Annual meeting attended by all managers, devoted exclusively to discussion of the culture.

Straight Talk

Senior executives explain reasons for current actions and decisions in freewheeling exchanges with associates that occur several times a year.

Kick-Off Meeting

A first-quarter road show that combines a celebration of the past year's achievements with a serious look at what lies ahead in the coming year.

ments with a serious look at what lies ahead in the coming year—and (of course) why. The Kick-Off themes are always developed from the issues raised on the previous year's Culture Survey. Every officer participates, and every associate is invited to attend one of the five regional versions of the show, either in person or via closed-circuit hook-up.

This communication assault on the organization has proven to be extraordinarily effective in advancing Rooney's change agenda. Leaders and associates may vary in how quickly they reach the stages of acceptance and commitment, but it is hard to find anyone in U.S. Cellular who does not have a very clear understanding of where the company is going, why it is essential to get there, and what it expects of its people in helping to reach that destination.

Leadership Development

Leadership development—training for leaders—has always been a vital part of Rooney's culture change portfolio. He asks his leaders to adopt what will for most of them be entirely new ways of getting things done. Even the most sympathetic among them will probably need help in mastering unfamiliar behavior patterns. It is only fair that they get every opportunity to learn how to fulfill the Dynamic Organization's requirements.

Rooney has been building a portfolio of leadership development programs, specifically tailored to make leaders effective within the culture, since his first days at Ameritech Cellular. The mainstay is the Leadership Development Workshop for front line leaders, an intense immersion into the D.O. Hundreds of U.S. Cellular leaders have looked back on their LDW experience as "the moment the light went on." The LDW is just one of a network of progressively more sophisticated programs designed to build effective leadership to the D.O's specifications. The New Leader Timeline lays out the first year's worth of training activities that await new U.S. Cellular leaders. (See *figure 2*, page 64.)

There is no doubt about the effectiveness of these programs. One typical new leader, freshly arrived from a competitor, pointed out in some amazement that he had been more thoroughly evaluated, more rigorously assessed, on-boarded in more detail, and given more constructive feedback in his first ten months than in his previous ten years in the business.

What is most striking about the development programs is the urgency with which attendees approach them. They are not the classic "nice-to-haves" of most companies, a welcome perk and a break from the pressures of the job. Instead, they hold the keys to the new order, critical information that leaders need in order to function effectively. The training is urgently driven by

FIGURE 2

a user demand ratcheted to high levels by the knowledge that leadership effectiveness—*their* effectiveness—is being tracked constantly through the Culture Survey.

For the first few iterations of the LDW, the importance of leadership training in the Dynamic Organization was underlined by Rooney's use of a pass/fail assessment at the end of the workshop to measure how well participants had absorbed its lessons. When word got around the company—and it did, in record time—that a few participants had in fact failed this assessment and lost their leadership positions as a result, leaders scheduled for upcoming workshops began to obsess about its life-altering importance. These failures were all leaders who had neglected to take the program, and the culture, seriously. Once the company had the laser-like attention of future participants, Rooney relaxed the pass/fail standard. From then on, however, no one at U.S. Cellular held any illusions that culture was not a serious matter worthy of their full attention. The company was playing this game for keeps. For the next few years, demand for prized slots in the LDW program far outstripped their availability, and even now there is continuous pressure to get new leaders into the program sooner and sooner.

Leaders are held accountable for their performance in two dimensions: the what *and the* how.

Talent Review

The Culture Survey, communication programs, and leadership development all generate masses of information and high levels of organizational awareness of the company's triumphs and challenges. The engine that converts all this input into positive change is the "Talent Review," Rooney's totally idiosyncratic take on leadership performance management.

The Talent Review is where accountability for leadership performance is assigned and assessed. The bland title belies the intensity of these proceedings—no surprise given the prime role assigned to effective leadership in the business model. When Rooney first introduced the process at Ameritech Cellular, it was quickly dubbed "the Star Chamber," a title Rooney approved of until he was persuaded that something a little less intimidating might send a more developmental message. In these sessions, Rooney's 20-member executive team reviews annually each of U.S. Cellular's 180 directors and vice presidents in a free-for-all discussion to which all members of the group are expected to contribute.

These leaders are held accountable for their performance in two dimensions: the "what" and the "how." The "what" includes their specific numerical results and project goals, and is just as important in the overall perception of the leader's effectiveness as at any other company. Any leader tempted to take an eye off the numbers ball is quickly reminded that U.S. Cellular, for all its devotion to values like respect and empowerment, is not a non-profit business.

The "how" assesses the way the leader gets those results. Do they happen through the tenets of the D.O., or in spite of them? Does the leader operate in harmony with the D.O.? Is he/she a cultural role model? In the discussion of the "how" dimension, each leader's direct reports get a vote, through the culture survey, that is just as important as the executive consensus. Kruger attends all Talent Review sessions to make sure this associate perspective is fairly weighted.

High-potential leaders excel in both the how and the why dimensions. They get superior results, and they do it the right way. Those who do neither have usually been asked to leave the business before they get to the Talent Review. Leaders who achieve the "what" without the "how" go on stringent performance plans, with tight time-frames. Making the numbers is no defense for failing to live the company's values. These leaders have to make significant, measurable strides to correct their shortcomings within 30, 60, or 90 days, depending on the severity of the problem.

The organization is more patient with those who are good cultural fits but fail to achieve their goals. Such leaders also find themselves on performance plans that focus on what they need to learn to translate their positive traits into results, but they are given more time to make the necessary changes. This is a reflection of Rooney's distinction between the "will" and the "skill" factors in leadership performance. If will is the problem—the leader is not supportive of the culture and not trying to operate within it—there is little

One of Rooney's mantras is that in order to transform a culture, there is just one fundamental choice: you have to either change people—or change people.

room for forgiveness. If, on the other hand, the issue is skill, Rooney will invest in the training and development needed to retain a leader whose values match the company's.

What is critical to the development of the culture is the equal importance placed on each of the two dimensions. Making good numbers is enough, in most companies, to ensure job security for bad actors of all kinds. Not here. Some of the most important of U.S. Cellular's culture-building legends describe the importance of "addition by subtraction"—how stores or call centers or whole regions see their performance take off when the "bad apples" are removed.

The outcome of the process is, quite literally, dynamic. The system permits no standing in place. Leaders are either meeting the effective leadership requirement of the business model, or they are held accountable for doing what they need to do to correct their deficiencies, or they have to leave. One of Rooney's mantras is that in order to transform a culture, there is just one fundamental choice: you have to either change people—or change people.

Many leaders who profess to want change balk at the second of these alternatives, allowing inadequate or insincere incumbents to remain in their positions, where they will inevitably sap credibility and energy from the change initiative. For Rooney, the culture is all-important; leaders who lack the qualities to make it work are a fatal liability that he will not allow to endanger the greater good.

It is this intense sense of urgency underlying all these tools for cultural change that makes Rooney such an effective implementer. In almost every other company that has attempted similar changes, there is a gut understanding in most employees that the initiative, no matter how boldly launched, is not entirely serious, that it is essentially ceremonial and superficial, that it will not survive meaningful and persistent challenge. The first bad quarterly earnings report, the first budget shock, the first serious conflict with friendship or engrained habit, and the new culture will fold; or if not on the first challenge, then certainly on the second or third or tenth. Sooner or later, the sponsors will decide that the pain is not worth the gain. They will declare victory anyway (perhaps marked by a face-saving celebration), and yet another flavor-of-the-month will be filed away in the institutional consciousness.

Rooney does not even understand that language. He has had for many years in the center of his desk a plaque that captures his credo perfectly: "It Shall Be Done." This is not a statement of power or ego, but of simple fact: failure to implement is simply not an option. It will not likely be easy or cheap, and it may take longer than anyone expects, but it shall be done. Change people—or change people.

PART 2

Building the Dynamic Organization

FIRST THINGS FIRST:
THE CUSTOMER

The customer's primacy should be a truism in any retail organization, but in the wireless telephone industry at the turn of this century, "the customer" carried surprisingly little weight. After a decade of wild expansion, during which cellular companies had become accustomed to double-digit annual growth, customers were a dime a dozen. Providers held all the cards: a technology that had captured the popular imagination, addictive gadgets that got smaller, more feature-laden, and "cooler" by the month, industry-friendly regulations that forced consumers to play by the carriers' rules if they wanted to board the wireless bandwagon, and a huge American market that was still far from saturated.

With customers lined up to get into their stores, no cellular company paid much attention to how they were treated once they signed up. If that resulted in increasing customer frustration with unreliable service, hit-or-miss product quality, and indifferent provider responsiveness, well, who was going to miss a few thousand pain-in-the-neck subscribers with unrealistically high expectations? The idea of investing in improving customer service for people who were already in the fold seemed foolish, an unnecessary drain on the bottom line.

Meanwhile, the wireless industry was developing a nasty reputation. Consumer polls made it clear that these companies had managed to create a frustrating and generally unpleasant experience. Dealing with one of the cellular giants was about as edifying as coping with an airline. Churn rates rose to levels that would have been alarming if not for that seemingly endless supply of not-yet-disillusioned new customers.

U.S. Cellular was not much different than its bigger competitors in those days, except that it had fewer customer-pacifying toys to offer. What reputation it had was as a reluctant spender that excelled in achieving bottom line results, a quintessentially numbers-focused organization. Its headquarters-based managers rarely met a customer and (because U.S. Cellular did not yet operate in Chicago) had no first-hand experience of dealing with their own company.

"Customer service" was a necessary evil, an expense that created more headaches than opportunities. Much of it was provided through call centers where poorly paid, ill-trained, and under-equipped associates spent as little time as possible before moving on. Annual turnover in U.S. Cellular's call centers approached a staggering 80 percent. Several of them found it necessary to measure a behavior almost unheard-of elsewhere: "job abandonment," where fed-up service reps simply drop their headphones, head for the door, and never come back, not even to collect a final paycheck. In one particularly troubled center, the annual abandonment rate often approached 20 percent of the workforce.

The welfare of the company's customers was rarely top-of-mind for employees working in this environment. There were many exceptions, of course—service reps with an instinctive desire to help people, or just to do a good job. Still, the biggest reason for whatever "loyalty" its customers did demonstrate was the lack of an alternative. U.S. Cellular thrived in third-tier and rural markets that had not yet piqued the interest of the industry giants, preoccupied as they were at that point with harvesting the easy profits of urban centers. Most of its customers had little or no choice if they wanted to sample the wireless experience. They stayed with U.S. Cellular because they had to—for the time being, at least.

That was the situation when Jack Rooney became U.S. Cellular's CEO. Everything about it struck him as absurd. Why would any company—let alone a small player struggling to find a viable position in an industry ripe for consolidation—squander its most precious asset?

Now Rooney had an opportunity to apply once more the ideas that had worked so well at Ameritech. As he outlined the Dynamic Organization to skeptical U.S. Cellular audiences in the winter and spring of 2000, the centerpiece of his vision was the customer, and the critical strategic importance of customer satisfaction. U.S. Cellular would be the company that best understood its customers and their needs. At a time when other companies were aloof or indifferent or downright hostile to customer expectations, U.S. Cellular would raise them. If customers were wondering where they could turn for satisfaction and relief, U.S. Cellular would open wide its arms. In return, those customers would reward the company with their business and, more importantly, their loyalty. Customer loyalty would be the key, not just to survival, but to long-term prosperity.

As he barnstormed the company, Rooney concluded every session by teaching his associates a new battle-cry. "Customers expect it," he would shout. "And we deliver!" the audience would shout back. There was in these first iterations of the chant that would reverberate across the company for the next eight years a substantial measure of wishful thinking. U.S. Cellular was little better than its peers in keeping its customers happy. But that cry, repeated with increasing conviction over the months and years, drew a line in the sand, one that clearly distinguished the company from its rivals, and one that provided at least the outlines of a viable path to the future.

At a time when other companies were aloof or indifferent or downright hostile to customer expectations, U.S. Cellular would raise them.

When these associates allowed themselves to hope that their company just might find a route to survival, customer service was the beacon that encouraged them. Of the five Values that Rooney described as the foundation of his Dynamic Organization, customer focus was both the most concrete and the most important. Empowerment and ethics and respect and pride might seem like somewhat nebulous wish-list items, but customer focus was a clear and present imperative, one that the new CEO was quite obviously unwilling either to compromise or to defer. From the beginning, the one thing for which there was no excuse in Rooney's U.S. Cellular was failing to put the customer first.

The customer's strategic importance to U.S. Cellular was clear to associates as soon as Rooney articulated it. It was the only way a company like U.S. Cellular—small, diffuse, and with few of the material resources of its rivals—could survive, let alone win. The "Ideal Customer Experience" generated by a passionate, energetic, determined work force was the only potential competitive advantage available to an underdog company. If U.S. Cellular could move into the satisfaction void left by its arrogant, insensitive competitors, it might be able to create a sustainable niche for itself.

THE CUSTOMER AS TROJAN HORSE

The Dynamic Organization envisions a body of associates who have moved beyond pure self-interest, who have subsumed their personal concerns into a larger cause: contributing to a team that succeeds by helping others. This endeavor engenders pride and personal growth, and it is deeply rewarding in ways that go far beyond the conventional economic trade-offs of the workplace. Its success depends on associates being able to make perhaps the most fundamental psychological change of all: a shift from the "what's in it for me?" stance that is so basic to our society and economy to a genuine interest in and empathy for others. It would be a tough sell for any new CEO to convince employees—especially in a ruthlessly competitive sales environment—that their self-interest is best served by subordinating it to the ethical and respectful treatment of their co-workers, their leaders, and the community at large. In most retail organizations, such a program would seem hopelessly naive, totally disconnected from the harsh, me-first, elbows-out realities of the American marketplace. But if that request were prefaced by a solid business case for putting the customer on a pedestal, together with a plan for making it happen, it might at least get their attention. And if the plan worked—if customers reacted positively and showed their appreciation in tangible ways—bottom line success might confer credibility on the new approach. What had initially seemed outlandish might then look like it was at least worth a try.

> *"The most important people in the company are the ones you choose to talk to your customers."*
>
> —JACK ROONEY

Rooney had seen at Ameritech that even associates who were hostile to change in general had a soft spot in their hearts for their customers. While that was not surprising among the descendants of Ma Bell, he saw the same kind of instinctive customer empathy in his U.S. Cellular ground troops. Many of these sales and service reps sympathized with their customers, even when, under their previous management, they had been unable to do much to help them. One of the most debilitating aspects of their jobs, in fact, was finding themselves caught between the usually conflicting desires of their customers and their employer. If that conflict were removed—if the customer's interest and the company's could somehow be made to coincide—their work would be far more rewarding and satisfying than it had been.

The customer, in other words, could be employed as a kind of Trojan horse to undermine resistance to culture change, capturing the hearts and engaging the enthusiasm of associates far more quickly than abstract (at this point) concepts like "effective leadership" or "superior business results." Once associates' underlying empathy for customers was engaged, it might gradually be expanded to win associates over to the less accessible values and behaviors of the Dynamic Organization.

That was Rooney's plan for U.S. Cellular. His workforce in 2000 was far from ready to take on the Dynamic Organization as a whole. In his call centers, it was not at that point safe to leave a lunch-bag in a communal refrigerator, and many sales reps felt justified in compensating for skimpy compensation by helping themselves to inventory. But his appeal to Customer Focus struck a chord. Treating customers fairly was something that even a small company could do, if it worked hard enough, and get immediate positive feedback for the effort. The approach played especially well in U.S. Cellular's small-town and rural strongholds, where friendliness was already an entrenched virtue. This new emphasis on Customer Focus just brought the company's official position into alignment with the natural order of things in those communities.

Customer focus was an immediate hit at U.S. Cellular, and not only among associates. Customers noticed too, and showed their appreciation by allowing the company to record industry-best churn rates. Monthly churn dropped below 3 percent by mid-2001, and stayed there, continuing to decline until it broke the 2 percent barrier by the end of 2005. If the rest of the industry continued to treat subscribers with indifference (or worse), at least one company offered them a safe haven.

Once established as a winning formula, the primacy of the customer became a wonderful organizing principle for broader changes within the company. It set standards: the ability to see the business "from a customer's perspective," to "visualize the Ideal Customer Experience," and to implement that vision "relentlessly and zealously." Leaders and associates began to sort themselves out according to their willingness to accept those standards and their ability to achieve them. Those who fell by the wayside were replaced by others who were attracted by the vision and had the skills to execute it.

Gradually, the company began to change. When acceptance of the value of customer focus led to irrefutable business results, the way was opened for other components of the D.O. that had at first seemed more rarified. Maybe empowerment and openness and common purpose and trust were not such wildly impractical concepts after all. The initial success of customer focus helped transform the other values and desired behaviors from lists of words that had to be learned to demonstrate orthodoxy into practical steps that would help deliver a superior customer experience.

Empowerment is a prime example. It is, perhaps, the most abused management concept of the past half century. For many managers, the word conjures up nightmarish images of inmates running the asylum, while their employees have come to see it as a trap designed to leave them holding the bag when things go wrong. For Rooney, though, empowerment of the front-line associate is essential to the quality of the customer's experience. The associate needs to be creative enough, sensitive enough, trained enough, and confident enough to make on-the-spot decisions that will meet or exceed the customer's expectations.

Seen from the perspective of customer focus, empowerment sheds its connotations of abdicating managers and set-up-to-fail employees. It becomes a critical tool in delivering the company's new stock-in-trade: world-class customer satisfaction. Empowerment, in this light, is not about the associate, but about the customer. In this way, customer focus rapidly converted empowerment at U.S. Cellular from a vaguely understood buzzword to sharply defined essential. Within two years of Rooney's arrival, the critical importance of the empowered front line associate was an article of faith at U.S. Cellular.

Empowerment is not about the associate, but about the customer.

In the beginning, many associates regarded ethics as an optional extra—desirable perhaps, but largely irrelevant to the Darwinian world of sales and service. The light went on, little by little, through the lens of customer focus. For many customers, the critical difference between U.S. Cellular and its competitors was the simple fact that they did not have to watch their backs during their transactions with the company. Customers loved the fact that they could assume that they would not be taken advantage of, and that if they had a problem with their service the company would deal with it honorably and conscientiously. This feedback was so consistent that associates came to understand that the ethics value—far from being an obstacle or a distraction or an irrelevancy—had become one of their most valuable assets in building long-term customer relationships.

Diversity became the sixth Dynamic Organization core value in 2005. The culture was mature enough by then that most U.S. Cellular associates accepted diversity as a logical extension of the respect value, or even as an ethics-based imperative. Some, however, were concerned that the new addition might be a corporate expression of political correctness, and others were alarmed that it might signal a relaxation of the company's hiring and promotion standards. What won them over, to the point of near-unanimity by 2007, was the dawning awareness that diversity—whatever its merits as an independent concept—was vital to the customer experience. The realization that some customers might not feel welcome in a store where no one looked like them, or spoke their language, or shared their outlook not only made perfect sense; it shocked the organization to realize that not every member of their communities might immediately and automatically recognize their company's commitment to customer focus. That realization sealed the deal for diversity at U.S. Cellular, not just as an expression of goodwill, but as a practical necessity in a customer-focused organization.

It was customer focus that legitimized the whole notion, so critical to the Dynamic Organization, that "how" is just as important as "what" in judging the performance of both individuals and the company as a whole. U.S. Cellular could not win as a "what"-driven business defined solely by its numbers. Its best hope was to build an identity that went beyond the numbers, that appealed to customers in a way that its bigger, richer competitors could not match (or even, perhaps, comprehend).

That did not mean ignoring the numbers. They would always be critical indicators of whether the strategy was working or not. But the "what" would necessarily be subordinate to the "how." What mattered most would be how customers were treated in their transactions with the company, how leaders interacted with their associates, how associates approached their work each day. If all those "hows" consistently reflected the Dynamic Organization's Values and Behaviors, Rooney believed the company could do more than survive, more even than create a sustainable niche for itself. If U.S. Cellular were able to bring the D.O. to its fullest expression, it just might influence, if not transform, the way that organizations conduct business.

The company's initial acceptance of customer focus thus provided the door through which Rooney was eventually able to squeeze the rest of the Dynamic Organization's infrastructure. It provided the unifying framework for the entire cultural edifice that followed. It was because of their link to the customer that the other values and behaviors eventually emerged as an integrated whole, a coherent culture instead of a disconnected series of worthy initiatives.

PHASE 1: "LET'S SEE WHAT HAPPENS"

The transformation we've been describing was by no means instantaneous. No company of any size, no matter how willing, turns on a dime, and most are unable to turn at all. At the time, U.S. Cellular was relatively small compared to its competitors, but that did not necessarily make it more flexible. Its employees were scattered to the four corners of the country, and, consciously or not, they were as inhibited by the habits and patterns of their existing corporate culture as the most hide-bound behemoth.

The U.S. Cellular Jack Rooney took over in 2000 certainly appreciated its paying subscribers, but these customers were not what made it tick. The company made most of its money indirectly, from the customers of other companies traveling in U.S. Cellular territory and forced to roam on its towers. In this way, the company's off-the-beaten-path locations provided a reliable windfall, at least for the short term.

This easy, "toll-booth" revenue came at a cost, however. With more money to be made through the cunning location of its cell sites than from providing service directly to its own customers, U.S. Cellular's focus was predominantly on its own financial well-being. Its executives' prime expertise was in extracting the maximum profit from the minimum investment, skills which had enabled their company to exceed fiscal expectations for years. Most of them were out of touch with their customers, and with the associates who served them. Prior to 2000, Chicago-based executives were rarely seen in their distant markets, which some of them had taken to referring to as "flyover zones." The closest many associates had been to their leaders was 30,000 vertical feet.

This was the audience for the new gospel of Customer Focus. Its first reaction, especially among the front line sales and service associates, was cautiously hopeful. The primacy of customer focus moved them from the periphery of the business to center stage. If their CEO meant what he said, the company was undertaking a radical change in its money-making strategy. Instead of relying on the financial wizardry of its headquarters-based managers, it was putting its trust in the ability of its field force to win the one-on-one battles for the allegiance of their customers. Most of these front line associates were thrilled with the new importance assigned to them and eager to explore the opportunities that came with this responsibility.

At the same time, the reality of their work environment

was so far from Rooney's vision that common sense suggested, at the very least, a wait-and-see approach. Their company's cautious, bottom-line-first instincts were so deeply rooted that associates found it hard to imagine that it would invest in the tools it would take to change customer relationships. And what would happen when the new approach hit one of the bumps in the road that were inevitable in such a volatile, competitive industry? Everything they knew about their employer suggested that if a favorable quarterly financial report were ever in jeopardy, if the numbers ever looked seriously out-of-whack, the new vision would be quickly jettisoned for a return to the tried-and-true.

The first Culture Survey, conducted in the summer of 2000, a few months into the new regime, captured this ambivalence in full bloom. The company's mood was upbeat. Most people liked Rooney's message, although some were upset by his insistence that change was necessary at all, and others resented the importance he seemed to place on concepts that seemed to be no more than common sense, values that most people should have learned as kids. Still, the vast majority were enthusiastic about the new direction. Whatever quibbles they might harbor about the details, at least it was a plan. Yet even the most optimistic supporters of the new regime expressed caution in their survey responses. Hundreds of write-in comments echoed the mixed feelings of the participant who wrote, "Sounds good; let's see what happens."

Their skepticism was justified. The 2000 survey revealed just how wide the gap was between the uplifting words of the Dynamic Organization and the current reality. Focus group participants, for instance, were asked what they thought their company valued most. The clear number one choice was "profits," with "customers" a well-beaten second. "Challenging" was the most frequently chosen adjective to describe the company, closely followed by "casual." (Rooney had abolished the company's dress code the previous month.) "Customer-focused" came in a distant third. When asked what single thing they would change about U.S. Cellular if they could, they generated a list that was overwhelmingly internally focused, split between hygiene issues like more competitive pay and benefits, and fundamentals of the work environment like better communications and training. Only two of the top fifteen items on this list directly benefited customers: providing better network coverage (eighth) and delivering better, faster, "one-call" service from the call centers (twelfth). Another segment of the focus group interviews called for participants to talk about what was the most and least fun about their jobs. The clear winner on the "least fun" side of the ledger was "angry customers."

The survey provided plenty of anecdotal evidence that the company was more focused on its own well-being than that of its customers. Field technicians complained about the brutal pressure they faced in meeting end-of-month or end-of-quarter deadlines to turn on new cell sites. Their mandate was "whatever it takes"—safety-endangering 20 hour days, for example, or costly temporary generators and microwave hops—to get the targeted sites at least nominally in service. Their complaint was not that such extraordinary effort was being expended, but that it had nothing to do with helping the customer. The real motivation for these regular deadline-induced frenzies was an informal adjunct to the compensation plan for engineering managers, which promised hefty bonuses for meeting their build targets.

Customer Service representatives in the call centers reported a similar complaint. Although their jobs nominally existed to help customers, their performance was judged almost exclusively on the basis of how close they came to efficiency and adherence targets. Hitting these numbers, they said, was far more important than satisfying their customers. As one rep put it, "You can hurt your team by helping customers."

Even if cultural barriers like these could be overcome, the company faced an even more daunting problem: an across-the-board shortage of the basic tools that a quantum leap in customer satisfaction would require. The company's habitual reluctance to spend had left it embarrassingly short of almost everything. Only a handful of its retail stores and none of its hundreds of kiosks had laptop computers. Inventory shelves were sparsely stocked, with customer selection limited, in practice, to the few models each store might actually have available. The Marketing department was understaffed and lacked even the rudimentary instruments to support a customer-based selling strategy. Field network technicians were required to share what tools they had. The list of what was missing, if the company were truly serious about putting up a fight for the customer, seemed endless, extending well beyond the bounds of realistic expectation. Many associates had to agree with the skeptic who appended a cautionary note to his approval of Rooney's agenda: "But wait till they find out it costs money."

That the reality of Customer Focus was in 2000 a long way from the shining promise of the Dynamic Organization was most of all apparent to the customers themselves. The typical customer experience with U.S. Cellular was discouraging: a long wait in an understaffed store, few product choices (none of them "cool"), a confusing hodge-podge of local calling plans, spotty and unreliable coverage, and the likelihood that subsequent inquiries would be handled by an inexperienced, poorly trained, and distracted service rep.

It would have been easy to look at this picture of U.S. Cellular and conclude that Rooney's plan to turn this company into a customer-delighting paragon was delusional. But there was promise as well. Rooney's vision had provided a glimmer of hope where there had been none. While the obstacles were obvious to everyone, the Dynamic Organization at least provided a map—not just a way out of the present impasse, but a route to a successful future that few had thought possible.

There was something else, as well. Along with the cautiously balanced hope and skepticism, there was an organization of people who were now at least trying to do something to improve their company's relations with its customers. There was evidence in this first survey that these associates were starting to build a self-image as people who cared more about the customer than their competitors, and as a company that, for all its shortcomings, at least wanted to do what was right for its customers. This was a seed that, with nourishing, just might blossom into something that wireless customers had never experienced before.

PHASE 2: COMING OUT OF THE CUSTOMER CLOSET

That first year of imminent change was, in retrospect, like the slow ascent of the roller coaster to the top of the first big rise, a mix of anticipation and foreboding and speculation about what the ride ahead would be like. And then—slam!—the headlong plunge that takes your breath away and has you holding on for dear life, simultaneously exhilarated and wondering how much more you can take, a wild ride that lasted, in this case, for years.

Every process, every policy, every assumption was up for grabs, judged by the sole criterion of whether it advanced the cause of customer satisfaction. Did call center associates need better training and more hands-on leadership? Double the number of supervisors, move them out of their offices, and put them in the middle of the action on the floor—and, in case the message failed to register, change their titles to "coach." Was high associate turnover preventing the development of strong customer relationships? Address every conceivable hygiene and environmental issue until your stores and call centers are industry showcases. Are decision-making executives too remote from the customer? Decentralize the company so that decisions are made on a regional basis, and, while you're at it, buy struggling industry rival PrimeCo, to provide a Chicago franchise and put U.S. Cellular phones in the hands of headquarters staff. What about the decrepit network held together largely by hope and prayer? Rebuild it to new standards designed to make U.S. Cellular service the most reliable in each of its markets. Are rate plans too fragmented and expen-

Every process, every policy, every assumption was up for grabs, judged by the sole criterion of whether it advanced the cause of customer satisfaction.

sive for customers to understand, let alone embrace? Chuck them all, in favor of a single, company-wide price plan, and offer national plans to compete with the giants.

This list of very real questions and their very big, complex, and frequently expensive answers could go on for many pages. Nothing went unexamined and little went untouched. While not every solution worked perfectly, the whirlwind of activity soon laid to rest the question of the company's willingness to invest in change. Associates came to appreciate a new quality in their organization: the courage to tackle any project, no matter how daunting, as long as it served the interests of the customer.

"Jack is trying to drive our little Volkswagen as if it were a Porsche."

—2001 Culture Survey
respondent

The sheer magnitude of change created for many associates a scary and explosive mixture of excitement and exhaustion. The prevailing sentiment on the 2001 Culture Survey was "What a difference a year makes!" Another participant that same year chimed in that "I've never seen a company change so fast." One caught the exhilarating nature of the ride by worrying that "Jack is trying to drive our little Volkswagen as if it were a Porsche."

A year later, the unrelenting pace felt "like changing tires at 100 miles an hour," and the use of the word "chaos" to describe the work environment became more prevalent. By 2003, it felt to many associates as if the company were trying to "sprint a marathon," and the deteriorating work/life balance of associates who had been driving change for three solid years started to become a serious concern.

What made the enormous effort worthwhile was the clear

evidence of genuine transformation. Everything that had been broken, all the problems and deficiencies that had been a constant reminder that U.S. Cellular was a second-tier player and a probable casualty of industry consolidation were being fixed. Rooney and his executives were doing what they said they would do. "What Jack promised is actually happening!" rhapsodized a 2001 survey write-in.

All of this effort coalesced around the customer. "Everybody's gone crazy for the customer," remarked one amazed participant in the 2001 survey, "even the janitors and the bean counters." "Now it's okay to be customer-focused," wrote another. "Before, you had to be in the closet." The associate who that same year wrote that "We've got 6,000 customer service reps now" reflected not only the extent to which customer focus had taken root, but the company's healthy growth rate.

Within only a year or two, the customer had become firmly lodged in U.S. Cellular's consciousness. Decisions that in the past would have been based solely on internal calculations were now generally preceded by the question, "What will our customers think?" "The customer is in the language now," confirmed one 2001 survey participant. Beginning in 2001, "customer focused" was by far the most popular entry in the "most descriptive words" section of the survey, as it would be every year thereafter.

Associates could see for themselves what a salutary effect customer focus was having on their company, and not just in the marketplace. One of their biggest complaints about U.S. Cellular in the past had been that it was a determined "follower" in almost every category of corporate performance. Now, at last, their company had staked out an area where it had made a public commitment to be a leader in the industry. Not only that, but it was making good on that promise with a determination that they had never seen before. Whether Rooney's grand plan worked or not, this ambition itself was something to be proud of, something that might, at last, set their company apart. As early as 2001, some survey participants were daring to think that customer service could, as one wrote, "make us a legend in this industry."

Hold-outs and Stragglers

As striking as these changes were, they were not universal. While the front line Sales and Customer Service organizations had adopted the customer satisfaction mantra with enthusiasm, associates in other parts of the company remained skeptical. The Engineering and Information Services groups in particular—led by old U.S. Cellular hands who regarded Rooney as an interloper and his Dynamic Organization as "rah-rah" gimmickry—tried to stand aloof from the change. Their leaders thought that if they could get Rooney the good survey numbers he seemed to prize, their tenure would give them enough leverage to keep the new culture at bay. And so for two years, these departments were bribed (one Network Engineering unit was renowned for conducting the survey during a two-day beer bash) or intimidated into generating survey results that would provide camouflage for a defiantly unchanging status quo. These practices ended with the departure, in 2002, of both department heads, but their resistance had created a time warp between the technical core of the company and the rest of the organization that would not be resolved for several years.

Something similar—although for less sinister reasons—was happening among the headquarters-based associates in Chicago who handled staff functions like Finance, Marketing, and Human Resources. Rooney's unrelenting championing of the customer-facing front line organizations seemed to many staffers to be a slap in the face. Long used to calling the shots at U.S. Cellular, these groups now found themselves expected to play a support role, an unwelcome change that was carved in stone when the name of their location was changed, in a 2002 reorganization, from "headquarters" to the "Regional Support Office," or RSO. Worse, they had to endure the CEO's repeated references to headquarters as the "etherdome." The heavier the load they shouldered during the marathon change process, the less funny they found the joke. By 2003, Rooney's teasing epithet had become in several instances self-fulfilling: these departments were working hard to bring the company's infrastructure into the 21st century, but felt isolated and cut off from the cultural progress their work was making possible.

"Two Steps Forward, a Step and a Half Back"

The customer experience itself showed how far the company still had to go. "The wait" was proving to be a persistent problem, something that customers, no matter how happy they were with their service, had to steel themselves to endure whenever they went to a store. It was a tribute to the loyalty the company was beginning to build that customers were willing to wait an hour or more for service in a busy location, but it was also clearly an intolerable problem that somehow resisted solution. Limited phone selection and a convoluted repair process continued to be customer irritants as well.

Still, it was obvious to everyone—including its competitors—that U.S. Cellular was making huge strides in putting the customer first. The service issues that had seemed too big and intractable to solve in 2000 were getting better, processes were more efficient, better tools were beginning to make a difference, and the sustained hard work of thousands of associates was gradually moving "the little engine" up that steep, steep grade.

"Everyone's gone crazy for the customer now— even the janitors and the bean counters!"

—2001 CULTURE SURVEY RESPONDENT

Most important of all, U.S. Cellular's self-image as the wireless company that does the best job of taking care of its customers was solidifying. During these first few years of the Dynamic Organization, it became an article of faith among associates that, whatever internal issues the company had yet to solve, two things were certain: a flawed customer experience at U.S. Cellular was still far better than its counterpart elsewhere, and someone, somewhere within the company was working to improve each of the imperfections.

This last certainty may have been reassuring, but it also meant that much of the company, as 2003 wound down, was approaching a state of exhaustion. That year's Culture Survey revealed signs of frustration. The previous three surveys had each shown modest improvement, and the results were generally good enough to be the envy of almost any company in the country. But the organization had not yet experienced the breakthrough that Rooney was looking for: the unmistakable sign that the whole company was unreservedly committed to the Dynamic Organization. "Two steps forward, a step and a half back," was the resigned comment of one tired survey participant in 2003. Another provided the most concise assessment of the situation: "We've come a long way, but we still have far to go."

PHASE 3: BREAK-THROUGH

"What a difference a year makes." That comment, reprised from the first heady burst of change three years earlier, was the apt summary supplied by a focus group participant in the summer of 2004, a year when all the disparate pieces of the culture change puzzle finally began to fall into place at U.S. Cellular.

The Culture Survey, now in its fifth annual iteration, spotlighted the breakthrough. For the first time, the results on

SERVICE ABOVE AND BEYOND THE CALL

Riding the Rails

The customer was a state agency responsible for the rail transport of farm products. Much of its internal communication was to and from trains. To make sure that this new customer's experience would meet their standards, a team of U.S. Cellular engineers loaded their test equipment aboard a freight car and traveled the state's entire rail network at 15 miles per hour to check network performance.

Next of Kin

A long-time customer was hospitalized with a serious illness. Knowing that he had no immediate family, the staff of his local U.S. Cellular store decided to cheer him up with a visit after they closed for the day. At the hospital, they discovered that their customer was too ill for visitors, so they asked the nurse to tell him they were thinking of him. The nurse asked, "Who should I tell him was here?" They suddenly realized how absurd it must sound to anyone outside the U.S. Cellular family when they heard themselves answer: "His cell phone providers."

every one of the survey questions improved over the prior year, and by a substantial margin. Nearly everybody (94 percent of the participants) thought well of the company. Almost as many agreed that the company was "heading in the right direction." Pride in what the company was accomplishing was at an all-time high; so was confidence in senior leadership. And at the center of all this positive feeling was the customer, whose presence dominated every response and many of the participant comments. "Our thought processes have changed," said one. "We automatically think of the customer now. We don't need the posters anymore—it's like breathing, just the way we do things."

What happened to create so much good feeling, after years of what often seemed like wheel-spinning? One critical factor is that customers began to reciprocate all the attention the company had been paying them for the past few years. Business results were excellent that year. U.S. Cellular was approaching the five million customer milestone and service revenues had more than doubled since 2000, tangible proof at last that Rooney's strategy was working.

Associate confidence got a further boost that year when customers were finally allowed to retain their personal phone numbers when they changed wireless carriers. Industry wise men had been predicting the demise of smaller companies like U.S. Cellular when customers finally were freed of this shackle, but Rooney had been confident that years of customer focus would pay off for his company. He was right. On the day when "number portability" took effect, people were lined up outside U.S. Cellular stores waiting to sign up. When the dust settled, it was a clear winner: one of the companies to gain customers when they were given a free choice of carriers.

U.S. Cellular was becoming a presence in wireless. Ignored by the big national companies for most of its existence, it was gaining a reputation for being a fierce competitor in its core markets. Other companies were noticing how difficult it had become to dislodge a U.S. Cellular customer; its churn rate was by then the best in the industry, and improving every year. Independent testing revealed that its once-disdained network had almost overnight become the most reliable in most of its markets. Network technicians noted with pride that many of their counterparts at other companies kept U.S. Cellular phones in their trucks because of their growing reputation for performing under extreme conditions—even during natural disasters. (See page 98.)

Another key to that year's breakthrough was that almost everyone was now on board with the Dynamic Organization. There were still some individual holdouts, and the company was just beginning to come to grips with the challenge of orienting all the new hires who knew nothing about the change saga of the previous four years and who brought a variety of old baggage to the table. But there was no longer any large-scale resistance to the culture.

The most important conversion had taken place in the Engineering department, which not only accounted for about twelve percent of the company's associates, but, in its Network Operations unit, represented a key component of the all-important "front lines." Until 2002, the entire department had simply opted out of the Dynamic Organization, paying only whatever lip service was necessary to avoid direct confrontation with Rooney. That year, the unit's long-time

---

NOW *THAT'S* RELIABILITY!

We were completing this manuscript when the great Midwest floods of 2008 inundated Cedar Rapids, Iowa, and many surrounding areas. U.S. Cellular has a call center there, as well as a major engineering office, with a total of about 500 associates. Many of them volunteered for sandbagging duties. As a large group gathered for instructions, the emergency coordinator began by asking who among them had U.S. Cellular service. A number of hands went up, and the coordinator announced that they were in charge of their teams, because they had the only functioning wireless service in the area. In one of the most profound tributes to the soundness of Rooney's insight that results follow service, Iowa sales skyrocketed in the aftermath of the disaster.

The Cedar Rapids call center was spared water damage, but a lack of electricity forced it to close for three days. During that period, many of its 450 associates were understandably preoccupied by their own losses. When the center re-opened, the company anticipated that absentees would number in the hundreds, and that the four other call centers would have to continue to handle most of the customer call volume until Cedar Rapids was back on its feet. That first day, exactly ten people failed to report for duty. Local service levels hit above-normal almost immediately, and stayed there.

---

head was himself engineered into retirement. His replacement got two mandates from the CEO: bring the network up to the standards of a customer-focused company, and bring the department into the Dynamic Organization.

The story of how that happened is told in detail later in this book. Suffice to say here that it was a major turning point for U.S. Cellular when, by 2004, the department's conversion was complete, and engineers were adding their testimony to the Culture Survey. Performance Engineers and Network Techs had by then begun to track down call quality problems by visiting customers in their homes, something that they had never done in the past. Now they were thrilled to be in contact with customers, solving their problems and making lasting friends for U.S. Cellular. Field techs took great pride in doing their maintenance work at night, unlike their competitors, to avoid mid-day service interruptions. Two years earlier, they had fought bitterly against this infringement on their freedom to do things their way. Their front line colleagues noticed the change. One sales leader commented on the 2004 survey that "there's been a tremendous change in Engineering, in how they work directly with customers. It's unbelievable."

Something similar, if less dramatic, was happening in the staff departments as well. New leadership helped in some areas, but the biggest factor in the conversion was the gradual accumulation of critical mass, combined with the validation of the new culture provided by the marketplace. It was becoming harder to be an outlier as the Dynamic Organization developed momentum.

It was also obvious that the parts of the company that were most engaged in change were having the most fun. Headquarters groups noticed the infectious spirit emanating from the front lines and wondered why their own environments were so different. They wanted in on the action, and pressured their leaders to join the rest of the company.

By the middle of 2004, it was hard to escape customer focus anywhere at U.S. Cellular. One staff member, participating in that year's survey, expressed amazement at how the customer had seeped into her sub-conscious: "Thinking like a customer has become second nature. The customer always has a chair in our meetings." An associate from Marketing echoed the thought: "We put the customer in the room when we develop and implement products." Another summarized the impact of this "amazing focus on the customer" by concluding that "This is a completely different company than before."

After the breakthrough of 2004, the culture ascended even greater heights the next year. Rooney thinks that two straight years of numbingly positive results lulled some of his leaders into complacency. The result was a string of gaffes in early 2006 that not only shook associates' confidence, but made customers wonder, momentarily at least, what was going on at the company they had come to trust. The mistakes were all well-intentioned. One was the introduc-

"We automatically think of the customer now. We don't need the posters anymore—it's like breathing, just the way we do things."

—2004 CULTURE SURVEY
RESPONDENT

tion of a new policy intended to safeguard customer privacy. In outlining its importance, executives took an unnecessarily threatening tone with call center associates, creating a major furor that lasted the better part of a year. Another was the mishandling of the roll-out of the E-911 program (an incident described in greater detail later in this book.) The unintended negative consequences of all these initiatives offered an object lesson in the fragility of even the strongest cultures—and the importance of taking nothing for granted.

The 2006 Leadership Forum was a sobering event. Leaders left that meeting determined to get back to the basics of the Dynamic Organization and to renew their commitment to the ideal customer experience. Their success, and the strength of the customer as U.S. Cellular's guiding star, was evident in the record-breaking results the following year.

Customer Focus has become such a successful strategy for U.S. Cellular that its big competitors have been forced not only to notice, but to respond with customer-centric approaches of their own. For the past several years, at least three of the four national wireless carriers have made variations on the "best network" claim a centerpiece of their advertising—enraging U.S. Cellular associates who know that most of those claims rely more on clever wording than reliable performance and that none of those networks can compete with their own.

"Customer satisfaction" has entered the industry's vocabulary as well. Based on the ads, one would think that the customer has no better friend than a major wireless company. For at least three years, the fondest dream of many U.S. Cellular associates has been that their company would fight back in its own advertising, telling its story and making sure that customers understand the difference between talking the talk and walking the walk. In 2008, they finally got their wish, as U.S. Cellular for the first time linked its public image to its internal culture, building its advertising campaigns around the extraordinary—and genuine—customer focus of its people. Based on a study showing that U.S. Cellular's customers stayed with the company longer than those of any competitor, billboards across the country were able to claim "America's most loyal customers." Eight years after he first introduced it, Jack Rooney's vision had become a fact.

THE LEADERSHIP
FACTORY

Leadership is good. Unlike "management" or "supervision" or "oversight"—words that convey suggestions of inequality and, possibly, coercion—"leadership" has no negative connotations. It is how battles and wars, games and championships, fame and fortune are won. Strong leadership is the elixir that cures whatever ails teams, organizations, even whole countries—a medicine that, miraculously, tastes good to the followers who take it.

The appetite for learning about leadership is insatiable. Would-be leaders are unsung pillars of the economy, supporting whole industries dedicated to describing, teaching, and celebrating leadership. The business press annually devotes countless pages to the topic, leadership academies and foundations and conferences and roundtables flourish regardless of the state of the economy, and leadership gurus get rich.

In this leader-obsessed environment, it might not seem noteworthy that a relatively obscure, mid-size company like U.S. Cellular makes "Effective Leadership" the linchpin of its business model. While few organizations go as far as U.S. Cellular in celebrating the importance of leadership, there are certainly many higher profile companies with strong reputations for developing leaders. New entrants to the leadership sweepstakes seem to arrive with every issue of *Fortune* or *Forbes*. *Fortune* published a "Special Leadership Report," as we were writing this section of the book. It celebrates the emergence on its global "Top Companies for Leaders" list of newcomers like Whirlpool, American Express, and Liz Claiborne, all newly worthy of comparison with such perennial "leader machines" as General Electric and Procter & Gamble. On the surface, it seems unlikely that there could be much to learn about the topic from such an unexpected source as U.S. Cellular. There are, however, some essential differences between the brand of leadership demonstrated in Jack Rooney's Dynamic Organization and the conventional version practiced elsewhere.

Leaders—whether they operate in the boardroom, in the stadium, or on the battlefield—are generally considered to be those charismatic individuals who, whatever the odds, are somehow able to motivate their people to achieve an unlikely goal. The more difficult the goal, the greater the feat of leadership. When the goal seems virtually impossible, the person most visibly responsible for its attainment is assumed to be a great leader, whose habits are therefore worth replicating in any other goal-pursuing context. With luck, these great leaders will share their secrets with their admirers, perhaps between the covers of a best-selling book.

Because it is the impossible goal—turning around a bankrupt corporate icon, winning the Super Bowl, snatching victory from defeat on the battlefield—that captures the popular imagination, the successful leader's methods often get less scrutiny than the results. True leaders do whatever it takes to make them happen. Since the goals are invariably worthy, ends justify means. The most celebrated leaders—the Lombardis, the Pattons, the Iacoccas—are tough characters, so focused on winning that they sometimes ignore conventional standards of behavior. In fact, it often appears that they are able to accomplish so much because they are willing to break the social and organizational rules that bind lesser mortals. From "Nice guys finish last" to "Winning isn't everything, it's the only thing," leadership has commonly been defined as the ability to get it done, whatever the "it" may be.

This popular definition of leadership as an amalgam of ruthless efficiency, visible toughness, and a big ego gets reinforced daily. In a recent article, former Reagan speechwriter-turned-pundit Peggy Noonan retold an apocryphal story about former British prime minister Margaret Thatcher, in which Thatcher publicly (but amusingly) humiliates her cabinet ministers. The anecdote "captures her singular leadership style, which might be characterized as 'unafraid.'" Noonan concludes, rhapsodically, "She was a leader."

Maybe. Over time, followers have been encouraged to think that tolerating a certain amount of anti-social behavior is the price we mortals must pay for having our bacon periodically saved by some larger-than-life, self-absorbed hero. As long as these so-called leaders get results, they seem to be exempted from the mundane rules—such as treating others with respect—that the led live by.

This is not the kind of leadership Rooney is cultivating at U.S. Cellular. His leaders are expected, as they would be anywhere, to get the job done. Their company is a tiny underdog in an industry of behemoths, without its competitors' financial wherewithal. It depends on the superior performance of its people to compete. That kind of winning performance is the responsibility of its leaders, whose ability to deliver the goods is tracked and assessed rigorously. Getting results, however, is only half the story in the Dynamic Organization. How those results are achieved is equally important, with the "how" very specifically defined: "All the Values and all the Behaviors, all the time." A result that is achieved the wrong way—that is, in a way that violates the letter or spirit of the D.O.—does not count. Leaders would do better to fall short of a goal than to reach it unethically, or by taking advantage of a customer, or by treating peers or associates or even competitors with disrespect.

> *"Eighty percent of the failure in business is because of leaders. Yet 80% of the brunt of the failure is felt by the people who can't do anything about it."*
>
> —Jack Rooney

THE WHAT AND THE HOW

Demonstrating effective leadership at U.S. Cellular looks deceptively easy. No politics intrude, no bullies obstruct, open lines of communication beckon everywhere. On closer inspection though, it turns out to be much more challenging than in most other organizations. Leaders must "get it done" as aggressively as anywhere else; but they are held just as accountable for the "how" of their accomplishments as they are for the "what." This two-dimensional accountability meant that most of the people who had been considered high performers before Rooney arrived (because they were good at getting results) had to dramatically change their ways. Just "making the numbers" was no longer enough to buy job security. His leaders were also expected to make a positive contribution to the culture, and to be active role models for it. That requirement rendered egocentric, selfish, me-first leaders obsolete at U.S. Cellular. Margaret Thatcher would probably do poorly in this environment.

This concept—that there is more to business life than the bottom line, and more than one way to get there—is so unsettling that it took years for U.S. Cellular leaders to fully grasp it. The learning process accelerated when Myra Kruger began to explain what the company expects of its leaders by depicting it graphically. (See *figure 3*, page 108)

The vertical axis in her diagram represents the "what" dimension: the ability to achieve results, make the numbers, accomplish objectives, get things *done.* The horizontal axis marks the extent to which leaders model the Core Values and the Desired Behaviors—the "how."

In evaluating an individual leader, the "what" axis can be plotted by using whatever performance and production indicators best demonstrate his/her proficiency in getting things done. The "how" axis is based on follower feedback from the Culture Survey. Once the leader's position on both axes is determined, the intersection point of the two projected lines places her/him in one of the graph's four quadrants.

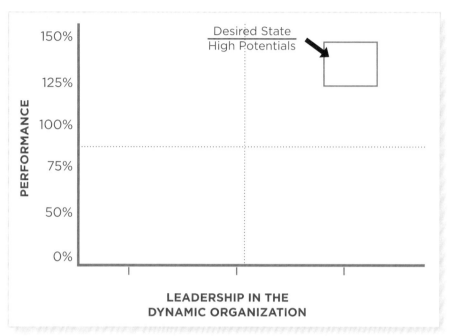

FIGURE 3

Leaders who are doing poorly on both dimensions find themselves in the lower left quadrant. They are making little contribution to the company from either a productivity or a cultural perspective. Without an immediate and dramatic turnaround on both aspects of their performance, they can expect their careers in leadership at U.S. Cellular to be short.

Leaders who fall into the lower right quadrant take naturally to the behavioral expectations of the Dynamic Organization and make strong contributions to the culture even though they may not be meeting the performance requirements of their jobs. The problem might be inexperience or a lack of training or a poor job match. These individuals are put on development plans designed to help them reach minimum production levels within a specified time frame. They are handled with a good deal of patience. Good cultural fits are not easy to come by, and the company makes every effort to put them in a position to succeed.

More problematic is the leader who falls into the upper left quadrant: the big producer who gets results in ways that are inconsistent with the Dynamic Organization—by cutting corners, or taking advantage of others, or failing to put the customer's interests first. In most companies, these people might be applauded, or at least left alone, their numbers gratefully accepted with few questions asked. In many, they shoot right up the corporate ladder, their momentum unhindered by non-numerical considerations. At U.S. Cellular though, they are put on a short leash, with a strict mandate to change their ways. Impressive results generated without the benefit of the values and behaviors are suspect, unlikely to help anyone—including the leader who produced them—in the long run.

The real leaders are found in the top right quadrant. They deliver a substantive "what" with an admirable "how." These are U.S. Cellular's high-potential superstars, the people who can solve any organizational problem, turn any troubled situation around, and raise any team's performance. Most of all, they can drive the company's unique business model. They get the desired results by enabling and inspiring their people to deliver a difference-making level of customer satisfaction.

What is most telling about the graph is how U.S. Cellular uses it. It is not just a static classification system for sorting out leadership strengths and weaknesses, nor is it merely a tool for identifying professional development needs. It assumes progress. Its underlying premise is that whatever the status quo, it is not good enough. Every leader has to be working to improve in one dimension or the other, striving to get out of the three bad boxes and into the good one. Those who are already in the good box need to keep moving, always heading toward the upper right corner.

While the double-axis chart has proved to be an excellent tool for clarifying the importance of both dimensions, it does not depict a critical fact about the relationship between the two elements: "how" comes first. It took years for most leaders to realize that Rooney was positing a causal connection between the two. They thought that "what" and "how" merely co-existed. Leaders were responsible for producing good results, and they were expected to get those results the right way. It only gradually dawned on the organization that getting the "how" right—all the Values and all the Behaviors, all the time—could actually drive the "what." Over time, the company noticed that leaders who were customer-focused, respectful, ethical, and empowering got more from their teams than those who struggled to represent the spirit of the Dynamic Organization. Gradually, leaders came to understand that embracing the D.O. was not just a "nice to have." It was an absolute essential, the key that would unlock a team's potential, the secret fuel that kept the "little engine" moving up an impossible grade.

Just as the "how" dimension determines whether leadership will be effective or not, leadership itself is the driving force in the Dynamic Organization Business Model. In fact, it is the only source of energy in that model, the only causal factor, the single point of entry. The model starts with effective leadership and moves in one direction only: from left to right, from leadership to associate satisfaction and commitment, and then from committed associates to satisfied customers, with those satisfied customers finally generating superior business results. (See *figure 1*, page 50.)

Many leaders, over the years, have challenged the logic of the Business Model, short-cutting one element or another to get to the bottom line. Some have tried to achieve associate satisfaction, for example, by buying it in one form or another, on the theory that pizza parties and ice-cream socials are an easier path to that destination than the company's uncompromising standards for effective leadership. The results of these campaigns have invariably done more to encourage associate entitlement than to benefit customers.

> *"This isn't a Chinese menu where you pick Value A from one page and Behavior C from another. This is all the values and behaviors all of the time."*
>
> —JACK ROONEY

Other leaders have tried to zero directly in on the customer, attempting to bypass the associate satisfaction segment, only to be harshly reminded that the state of mind of the front line associate ultimately shapes the customer relationship.

A few have tried to reverse the direction of the model, focusing solely on business results on the assumption that good numbers make everybody happy, associates and customers alike.

Wrong, all of them. Fifteen years of experience with the model underlines Rooney's insistence that it is a one-way street, with a single on-ramp, no short cuts, and an inevitable destination. That lone entrance point is the effective, two-dimensional leadership defined by the Dynamic Organization. Anything worthwhile happening in the organization can ultimately be traced to effective leadership. Where there are problems and obstacles in the way, that is also, with only very rare exceptions, a leadership issue.

It is this responsibility for the entire business model—the refusal to skip any of the intermediate steps on the way to business results, and the insistence that the model operates in a single direction—that distinguishes the brand of leadership practiced at U.S. Cellular from the conventional, just-the-results-and-don't-sweat-the-details leadership approach celebrated elsewhere.

Results-only leadership achieves goals, but has limited transformational power. It produces more and more of the same old stuff, and that is fine—if the same old stuff is what the organization needs. The traditional formula works well at many of the leadership icons cited by *Fortune*, where the driving imperative is "more and more" and there is limited interest in questions like "how?" or, especially "why?" The result, in such organizations, is often an admirably efficient vehicle with steering problems. Those defects are rarely visible, but are liable with distressing frequency to produce a sub-prime mortgage bubble, or an Enron, or an Iraq. When such disasters do occur, we are always amazed in hindsight at the damage wrought by what had seemed at the time to be "the best and the brightest."

The values-based leadership required by U.S. Cellular insists on examining the messy details implied by "how?" and "why?" It may be less efficient than the "no questions asked" variety. It is arguably slower. It took several years before U.S. Cellular was able to create the critical mass of leadership that made its Business Model viable. But once that happened, its young leaders demonstrated the capacity not only to reach their goals, but to go beyond the numbers to change lives for the better.

PHASE 1: TRIAGE

The transformation of U.S. Cellular from its former emphasis on the careful management of its assets to Rooney's vision of passionate, inspirational, caring leadership took time, evolving through several distinct stages.

Rooney began by putting the company he inherited in 2000 through triage, assessing the damage done by the prevailing "command without control" style of management, and trying to find enough leadership—within the organization or recruited from outside—to begin the transformation he envisioned. It was not hard to identify the most serious problems. Some important units had been allowed to drift into dysfunctionality. Several leaders, including a few key executives, had formed a resistance movement. A number of established cultural traits were completely at odds with the Dynamic Organization's definition of leadership. While some leaders immediately supported Rooney's declared intentions, none of them had any experience working in the kind of organization he was describing. As he looked around the company, he found plenty of potential allies, but very few leaders who were equipped to help with the enormous amount of heavy lifting on the immediate agenda.

Where to begin? An obvious candidate was the call centers which, despite an encyclopedic set of spirit-deadening rules and policies, bordered on anarchy because few of these rules were consistently enforced. Supervisors theoretically provided leadership to their teams, but their spans of control were huge—generally twenty-five or so service reps—and personal contact was rare. Offices located well away from the action on the call center floor, where a supervisor could shut the door and focus on the all-important paper-work, were a much-appreciated perk. Meanwhile, working conditions among the customer service reps, from the basics like pay and tools and training to higher-order needs like teamwork and recognition and pride were so primitive that annual turnover in some centers exceeded 100 percent.

Leadership was just as hard to detect in several of the company's fifteen sales markets, many of which were located in the country's farthest corners. Their remoteness, combined with the previous executive team's aversion to travel, gave local directors of sales virtual carte blanche to run their markets as they chose. A few did this very adeptly, guided by native leadership instincts that eventually made them assets to the Dynamic Organization. More common was the situation in a far west market, where the director of sales had built up a ghost payroll of cronies who had supposedly left the company, but who were actually still being paid while "working" out of a warehouse location known only to the director.

Sales reps in such markets felt, and often acted, like Dickensian orphans. Invisible to their company, uncared for by their supervisors, many of them operated under a law of the jungle in which "anything goes." (To judge by the depleted state of their inventory rooms, this was, in some cases, literally true.)

While leadership voids like these were all too common, even more distressing was the active antipathy to Rooney's approach on the part of several members of his inherited executive group. One vice president—a remote and forbidding individual with a regal manner that had earned her the mock-title of "the Queen"—seemed unable to get past the absurd notion that the Dynamic Organization countenanced "fun" in the workplace. Another had amassed personal control of every substantive decision affecting the company's network and technical domain, believed in pitting the major components of his organization against each other, and made it clear that Rooney's crucial first Leadership Forum would either have to wait until after duck-hunting season or get along without him. The vice president of another key technical function adopted an ostentatious pose of weary tolerance for what he judged to be yet another corporate passing fancy. He became a role model for passive aggression, effectively closing his department to outside influence. Most of the rest of the senior team was equally bemused by Rooney's expectations, but more politic in hiding their indifference. Even the most supportive among them were defensive about the implied criticisms of the old regime and unsure of how to go about fitting in with the new.

Associates across the company understood immediately the huge implications for their leaders of what Rooney was asking. One supervisor noted in a written comment on the 2000 Culture Survey that "This is a massive shift. Our whole job definition has changed. Every expectation is different." Associates saw leaders struggling to make the adjustment from remote, top-down managers of departmental silos in an environment where "we see our executives once a year, clap, and go back to work," to involved, passionate, inspiring role models for a culture that they could barely comprehend. Little wonder that so many of them seemed, as an associate observed, "confused, like they were caught moving in the wrong direction."

While the contrast between the old and the new expectations was dramatic, it was masked to a degree by the fact that the Dynamic Organization's vocabulary seemed at first to be deceptively familiar. Empowerment, for example, was far from a new concept; many U.S. Cellular leaders claimed that they were already practicing it. What the first Culture Survey made clear, however, was that this was in almost every case "empowerment by default"—the license for associates to do whatever they needed to do to survive that comes from absentee management, inadequate tools, and slack controls. "Most of the time," explained one front line associate, "you have no choice except to wing it."

The same argument was made about one of Rooney's most radical expectations: that communication between associates and leaders be characterized by openness and honesty. Almost no one took such a patently ridiculous goal literally. However changed U.S. Cellular might be, it was still, after all, a corporation, driven by power, organized by hierarchy, and run by people. What Rooney must be talking about, therefore, was the old open door policy, which many leaders felt they were already practicing. One call center director, for example, boasted of the sign she had placed outside her office offering an open door to all associates—every Tuesday between 1:00 and 2:00. In most cases, the reality was that while the door may have been literally open, when associates tried to bring their issues to their managers, in the words of one disappointed associate, "Nobody's there."

The case that the Dynamic Organization represented nothing new could be made (and often was, with much vehemence) by citing the familiarity of most of the new Values and Behaviors. Respect, ethics, pride, trust, unselfishness—these were ideals that most people learned as kids, the ordinary characteristics of decent people. Customer focus, empowerment and common purpose were just common sense concepts that any company should espouse. Several of them, after all, had been enshrined in U.S. Cellular's own two-year-old Vision and Values statement. How dare Jack Rooney act as if he had invented what was, at bottom, just a fancy-sounding version of the Golden Rule?

Leaders who thought this way often succumbed to a complacency that was just as disabling as the outright hostility of some of their peers. By trying to minimize the change represented by the Dynamic Organization, they justified the "wait and see" attitude that was so prevalent across the company in that first year.

Along with the active and passive resistors, there was a third group of leaders, a relatively small minority who welcomed the D.O. with open arms—either because they were frustrated with the limitations of the status quo, or because their personal convictions about people and organizations aligned with Rooney's, or just because they were drawn to the new sense of possibility that was slowly awakening in their company.

While the members of this group were welcome allies, most of them had no real idea of how to go about implementing the new approach. With no training programs in place and most of the company's infrastructure as yet unchanged, these early supporters of the D.O. were on their own, hoping that their instincts were carrying them in the right direction.

The results this vanguard produced were decidedly mixed. While some of them were winning the praise of their associates, the most obvious characteristic of these first efforts was their inconsistency. For every supervisor or manager trying hard to meet expectations that were still only vaguely understood, several others might be continuing on with business as usual, and a few more might be paralyzed by uncertainty. There was no reporting chain in the company where more than one or two leaders were on the same page. If a front line supervisor,

Leadership had become completely unpredictable. There was no reporting chain in the company where more than one or two leaders were on the same page.

for example, was trying hard to follow Rooney's lead, the next-level manager might be actively opposed to the new approach, while the director sat on the fence trying desperately to figure out which way the wind was blowing.

One of the most common associate comments on the first Culture Survey was the exasperated complaint that leadership at U.S. Cellular had become completely unpredictable. "Ask five different leaders any question, and you're guaranteed five different answers," went the refrain. Leadership changes were equally unpredictable. The chances of getting two good leaders in a row were slim. Even among those leaders who supported the Dynamic Organization, standards, expectations, and personal styles varied wildly.

One of the Culture Survey's most important contributions was to help the organization understand what, in their CEO's eyes, good leadership looked like. The sections that required participants to assess the leadership behavior of their supervisors and managers provided a detailed outline of Rooney's expectations. The results not only gave leaders their first formal feedback from the Dynamic Organization; they also helped both leaders and associates to understand the new expectations and to become familiar with a radically different vocabulary.

Those results started the arduous process of "winnowing" leadership—sorting the good from the bad, those with potential from those with no clue—that would be one of the hallmarks of the D.O. for the next eight years. Rooney had promised that the first survey would be for benchmarking purposes only, and he kept his word. No leaders lost their positions solely as a result of that assessment. Still, associates understood immediately the power of the survey, not only to drive the behavior of individual leaders, but to change over time the shape of the entire company. "Cull the bad and let the good rise," urged one perceptive participant in what remains the best short description of U.S. Cellular's development philosophy.

Some leaders had obvious potential to emerge, eventually, as stalwarts of the D.O. Few of them, however, were at that point the kind of strong, confident role models that Rooney needed to bring credibility to his approach, and they were getting no encouragement from the senior executives who were waiting for him to fail. The Dynamic Organization was facing an immediate leadership crisis before it was even off the ground.

Reinforcements from Ameritech

Rooney turned to some of his old Ameritech leadership team for help. Most of this group were unhappily employed by SBC after the takeover, adjusting with difficulty to working within the framework of a classic corporate bureaucracy. They had been "waiting for Jack's call," and were thrilled to get a second chance to be part of a Dynamic Organization. They provided an instant infusion of operational expertise and grounding in the culture.

This influx of seasoned leadership was accompanied by a tide of lower-level sales and service and technical associates who had been shocked at how quickly their culture had disappeared after Ameritech's demise. They made their own important contribution to U.S. Cellular, not only providing a healthy injection of talent, but sharing with their new colleagues valuable insights into how to navigate the Dynamic Organization.

These former Ameritech leaders provided a crucial bridge from the old U.S. Cellular to the new. It was a healthy sign of growing cultural maturity when, a year or so after the migration began, signs of resentment at the central role played by these leaders began to emerge. Associates and leaders alike urged the company to look harder at home-grown talent before tapping into the Ameritech connection. By 2002, it was not unusual to see Culture Survey comments to the effect that an Ameritech pedigree conferred an unfair advantage, and that "Jack's Ameritech buddies" had become a mixed blessing.

In the Dynamic Organization's formative first year, however, these imported leaders provided a lifeline for a company that had not yet made leadership development its signature competency.

PHASE 2: THE LONE RANGERS

Idaho's Snake River Valley—scenic and friendly, but decidedly off the beaten path—is an unlikely place to see the future unfold, but in the summer of 2001, when most U.S. Cellular leaders were still bewildered by their company's new direction, big things were happening there. The Idaho market, a string of small towns set along the river, was the company's smallest, and its out-of-the-way location made it even less visible than most. It was a money-maker, however, and as that year's Culture Survey approached and we prepared to go there for the first time to conduct focus groups, we were curious to see whether word of the Dynamic Organization had penetrated this far into the hinterlands.

The local director of sales, a pleasant young man named Nick Wright, was visibly nervous about his first in-person encounter with the new culture survey. Nothing in his manner prepared us for the raucous enthusiasm we found there. His team was a extraordinarily well-informed about the D.O., highly supportive of it, and generally far more advanced in building a customer-focused culture than any place we had visited in the previous year. They gave all the credit to Wright, the first home-grown leader we had met with a knack for "leading by inspiration, not by regulation." When the

Survey results came out that year, our in-person impressions were confirmed. Idaho was more positive about the Dynamic Organization and its own leaders than any other part of the company. This Nick Wright was clearly a name to remember.

Meanwhile, the company's East North Carolina market—a much larger area covering most of that state east of Raleigh/ Durham—was in terrible trouble. The key director of sales position had been a revolving door, business results were a significant disappointment, and associates in that summer of 2001 felt abandoned. Their Culture Survey input confirmed that the Dynamic Organization was at that point no more than a rumor.

The company's normal practice was to fill its open leader positions with a refugee from one of the big national carriers, but East North Carolina had churned up several of these retreads in recent years, to no avail. This time, Ellison decided to give his new star from tiny Idaho a chance. Maybe Wright would be able to translate his small-pond success to a much larger and far more troubled market.

As an experiment in growing the culture from within, the move was a roaring success. Within months Carolina attitudes had changed dramatically, and so had business results. By 2002, this market began a string of several years of chart-topping Culture Survey results, at the same time as it turned into one of the company's most reliable revenue generators.

Just as important as the results were the lessons learned about leadership. Rooney was right: effective leadership was the most important factor in success. A leader with the requisite qualities—a master of the "how"—could turn even the most troubled situation around and generate an admirable "what."

And such miracle-workers did not have to be imported from places like Ameritech. U.S. Cellular was, apparently, capable of producing leaders with the right stuff on its own.

Those lessons were reinforced in a much more negative way a year later. While East North Carolina gained momentum, Idaho's retrograde new leaders plunged that market into a decline that did not stop until U.S. Cellular divested it in a 2005 trade of properties that brought Kansas and western Nebraska in return. If effective leadership could solve any problem, it was just as clear that indifferent, self-centered, and unethical leadership could conjure up a disaster in no time flat.

While the Idaho/East North Carolina drama was unfolding, something similar was happening farther west. The Oregon/California market had a different kind of leadership problem. It was a fiefdom, largely ignored by a distant headquarters, run primarily for the personal benefit of the director of sales and his cronies. When associates used the Culture Survey to raise the alarm, the director was fired and his team decimated. The situation seemed as bleak as Carolina.

There were no obvious internal candidates to fix the mess, but there was one volunteer: Kathy Hust, a mid-level manager in the company's big Wisconsin market. Most of Wisconsin's leadership team remained non-committal, or worse, about Rooney and the Dynamic Organization, but the changes had struck a responsive chord in Hust, and she leaped at the challenge that Oregon represented.

Within a year, the former wasteland had blossomed into the company's best performing market, a showcase for the Dynamic Organization, and a leadership incubator. Here was further testimony to the power of Rooney's formula. All it took to clean up the most daunting mess was the kind of effective leadership he prescribed.

The same message emerged from the Customer Service side of the organization. The call centers were in much better shape than they had been when Rooney arrived, but the improvement was attributable mainly to the new resources he had given them: better training, smaller spans of leadership control, the attention of senior leadership. Most call center leaders were still struggling to find their balance between the numbers-orientation of the old era and the dangerous freedoms of the new. The dearth of leadership was so great that he again had to reach out to his old Ameritech network for help.

For the time being, the D.O. was overly dependent on a few heroes, Lone Rangers who, at the end of the day, would have to ride off into the sunset to save the next beleaguered town.

There was one encouraging exception: the Knoxville, Tennessee Customer Care Center was obviously a cut above its four counterparts, outperforming them statistically, but also displaying levels of understanding of the Dynamic Organization, engagement with the company's goals, and creativity in implementing them that set it apart. In focus groups, participants gave all the credit to Tom Catani, the center's director, himself a bright, curious, and creative leader who saw the Dynamic Organization as the answer to his prayers.

Catani showed that he had the right stuff for the new culture by his handling of an early payroll crisis. He had just been made acting director of the troubled Cedar Rapids call center in addition to his Knoxville responsibilities when he found himself in possession, on a Thursday evening, of every paycheck due the next day in Iowa. Since he seemed to be the only responsible adult connected to the Iowa center, the Payroll unit had decided to send him everything. The only problem was that he was in Knoxville at the time, and several hundred unhappy Iowans would within 24 hours be heading into a weekend without grocery money. Catani made the instinctive decision to hop in his car and drive the 675 miles between the two centers, arriving in time to assure a happy ending to the story.

Wright, Hust, and Catani—each of whom is now one of the company's four Regional Vice Presidents—were early symbols of great significance, offering living proof that Rooney had put U.S. Cellular on the right track. Just as important, they helped the company begin to put to rest its old inferiority complex. It had always assumed that the best leaders came from elsewhere, and especially from the big companies with national reputations. Rooney's early reliance on his Ameritech connection had done nothing to change that impression. Now here were people whose backgrounds were not very different than their U.S. Cellular peers', emerging from the pack to play key roles. If they could do it, why not others?

That heartening possibility, however, was still some distance in the future. For the time being, the Dynamic Organization was overly dependent on a few heroes, Lone Rangers with the will and the skill to rescue a situation, but who, at the end of the day would have to ride off into the sunset to save the next beleaguered town. When they left, there was still no telling what kind of leader would succeed them.

Clues from the Culture Survey

Most U.S. Cellular leaders were still trying, with varying degrees of success, to grapple with a bewildering set of challenges. By 2001, the company was raising the performance bar to undreamed-of heights, developing organization-wide standards, rebuilding its infrastructure, playing catch-up in a hundred different areas, and doing it all yesterday. This would have been an overwhelming agenda even if leaders were able to rely on the old reliable tools of their trade for getting things done: rules and regulations, threats and intimidation, directives backed up by fear. These methods had not worked particularly well, but at least they were familiar. Now Rooney was insisting that they abandon these old habits and lead in an entirely different way, "inspiring" their people to achieve great things instead of just telling them what to do. Few of these leaders had any idea of what that meant. They had never had to inspire anyone before, and certainly no one had ever inspired them. This was new territory, and they had few maps to guide them.

One source of helpful information was the Culture Survey. Each year the Esler Kruger report would catalog examples of leaders who, if they were not yet performing miracles, were winning the respect and loyalty of their teams. A director of sales set an example by routinely showing up at some store in his market half an hour before opening time on Saturday mornings, at a time when many store managers thought that weekends off were a perk of leadership. A call center director amazed her associates when, after a bomb scare had shaken the center, she spent the next forty-eight hours on the premises, reassuring her reps and talking her leaders through their fears. The director at another center had the same kind of impact by simply picking up a headset when her team was overwhelmed and taking customer calls until the crisis had passed.

These were mundane examples, but they gradually helped to piece together a picture of what inspirational leadership looked like. Such leaders put the welfare of their associates and their customers before their own; they led by example, not by directive; they got into the trenches with their troops, rolling up their sleeves to help in a crisis; they supported their teams, fighting for them when necessary; they were caring and humble; they helped their associates learn and grow. From these bits and pieces, leaders were encouraged to assemble an approach that could work for them.

Their progress, at this stage, was still painfully slow, like learning a new language by rote. Only a few "naturals" had successfully integrated the "how" of the Dynamic Organization with the "what" that overloaded their plates. For most, the two sets of expectations remained separate. The D.O.'s behavioral requirements were not yet making it easier for leaders to get things done, as Rooney had promised they would. Instead, they represented an additional burden, one more set of expectations on a list that was already much too long.

Still, by 2002, it was clear to almost everyone that U.S. Cellular's new direction was paying off. The company was expanding and its work force was growing. It had never experienced a lay-off, in an industry where such events were a regular sacrifice to the bottom line. It was not yet out of the competitive woods, but associates felt more secure than they had in years. For all those positive signs, however, most of the organization still thought of the D.O. as Rooney's baby, his vision, his responsibility. Its success or failure remained almost as dependent on him as it had when he was introducing it. There was little evidence that other leaders were assuming ownership of the culture, or that they considered themselves responsible for making it work.

All eyes were on Rooney. He can be a high-decibel communicator, especially with senior leaders, and every blow-up was noted, embellished, and passed around the organization for scrutiny. To the D.O.'s remaining enemies, these hiccups were opportunities to discredit the entire initiative. Every inflated example of Jack's yelling was used, in some quarters, to demonstrate his hypocrisy. How did that kind of behavior square with the value of respect? How could he expect his leaders to live the D.O. when Jack himself didn't walk the talk?

These episodes may have set the culture back in some ways, but they were also a sign that the company—even the least progressive parts of it—was paying attention. Associates were learning to observe leadership closely, to pay attention to the behavioral differences between the effective leaders who got results and made their teams feel proud in the process, and those who remained stuck in their old habits. They were not yet the connoisseurs of leadership that they would become in a few years, but they were watching, listening, and learning.

PHASE 3: DEMAND OUTPACES SUPPLY

The next stage in the emergence of U.S. Cellular as a leadership factory was actually a setback, a painful but necessary lesson that delayed the evolution of the Dynamic Organization by a year or more.

While the demand for inspiring, caring leaders who were strong enough to drive Rooney's business model was exploding, the supply was lagging. The success of the Lone Rangers had proved that the model worked, but only in the right hands. Their example had given many fledgling leaders inside the company the courage to take a chance on this new approach. This next wave was gaining experience and building self-confidence, but few of them were ready to become "D.O. heroes" in their own right. Meanwhile, the company's growth was creating enormous pressure to fill an expanding number of senior positions.

The Demise of "Brand Name" Leaders

The obvious answer was to hire experienced leaders from outside the company to fill the gap. At that time—2003 and 2004—U.S. Cellular still suffered from a lingering inferiority complex. Even though many associates were beginning to realize that their little company was out-performing its bigger, richer rivals on many levels, there was still a tendency to view the giants with awe. Anyone with a pedigree from AT&T or Verizon or Sprint was assumed to be a big catch. It still seemed like an honor when such a candidate deigned to notice U.S. Cellular.

In the excitement that inevitably followed whenever a big-company veteran appeared on the company's radar screen, few people paused to wonder why that individual might have become available. Even fewer considered that leadership roles and expectations in those companies were vastly different than at U.S. Cellular, and that this gap might be a significant hurdle. All that mattered was the name on the label.

Let the buyer beware. While some of these hires worked out well, the list of failures was long and imposing. Collectively, the brand-name stop-gaps did a significant amount of damage to the still-fragile culture.

These failed recruits had one characteristic in common: arrogance. They found it hard to believe that U.S. Cellular, long disdained by the industry when it was noticed at all, had anything to teach them. They were doing their new company a favor, not the other way around, even though several of them would not have had many other employment options. Those who bothered to notice that big changes were taking place within the company misread them. They tended to underestimate the Dynamic Organization as a soft and fuzzy distraction camouflaging the usual corporate lust for numbers.

U.S. Cellular was expanding into a number of new markets during that period: Indiana, Chicago, Omaha, Oklahoma City, Portland (Maine). The need for leaders in these locations was especially acute, and as a result, outside hires wound up running several of them. These newcomers got little in the way of orientation or mentoring. U.S. Cellular is a quintessentially can-do company, and its tendency at the time was to throw its senior recruits into the deep end of the pool and hope for the best. After all, these guys had played in the big leagues.

One of these big leaguers came out of retirement from AT&T to almost destroy the struggling Indiana market. He made two memorable contributions: he insisted on calling his sales team, against their ferocious objections, "Hoosiers" (many Indianans consider the term to be mildly derogatory), based on his apparently fond memory of the movie by that name about an underdog basketball team; and he made a habit of keeping open, during performance appraisals and other discussions in which a difference of opinion was likely to arise, the desk drawer in which he kept a handgun. He self-destructed in a cloud of ethics violations and personal controversy, but not before undermining any confidence his team might have had that U.S. Cellular was serious about the Dynamic Organization.

A less spectacular, but equally damaging, episode took place in Oklahoma, an important market that became even more critical with the launch of Oklahoma City. It was entrusted to a former Sprint manager who possessed a wealth of industry knowledge, an engaging personality, and the ability to convince people that he was overwhelmed with work without actually doing anything. After a year of persistently disappointing results, he was asked to leave, but not before the market nearly imploded.

Something similar happened in the huge Chicago market after U.S. Cellular bought PrimeCo, a struggling Chicago-based operation whose acquisition finally gave the company an operational base in its hometown. With the franchise came several hundred associates accustomed to a very different culture than the Dynamic Organization. This was the classic challenge of merging opposites. If ever a situation called for an energetic, inspirational leader and role model, this was it. After a couple of false starts, what the market got, unfortunately, was an industry veteran, a pleasant, knowledgeable gentleman who became legendary, if such a thing is possible, for his passivity. In a situation that above all demanded action, he could not have been a worse fit. His year in office turned out to be lost time for the development of the Dynamic Organization in a market that Rooney had singled out as critical to the company's fate.

The "Coke Guy" did not last long enough for many associates to catch his name. He was given a senior leadership role in the East Region on the strength of the marketing acumen he was presumed to have acquired in a long career in the beverage industry. The region was spared the inevitable death dance when, in his first month with the company, he revealed himself to be an avid, albeit clumsy, sexist.

The failed recruits had one characteristic in common: arrogance. Collectively they did a significant amount of damage to the still-fragile culture.

The bad-hire issue was not restricted to Sales. The Engineering group brought in a high-level technical leader from AT&T who may or may not have been brilliant. His talents were obscured, however, by his compulsive politicking and his ability to repel almost anyone who had to deal with him. He quickly became a polarizing figure, a distraction whose disruptive influence far outweighed whatever positive qualities he had to offer. His arrest on a morals transgression, and subsequent dismissal by the company, was considered by many of his colleagues to be an example of providential intervention.

There were others. The newly-established Financial Services (collections) department spun its wheels for years under the direction of a succession of misfits chosen for their expertise rather than their suitability for the Dynamic Organization. Another department suffered the same fate when its new vice-president, chosen to replace, at last, one of Rooney's executive team hold-outs, revealed a genius for disruption. Her antics kept a vital unit off-balance and distracted. These are just the most spectacular examples from a much longer list of conventionally qualified people who were unable to translate their skills to the U.S. Cellular environment.

Growing Pains

Some of the external recruits who joined U.S. Cellular during this period managed to survive, going on to make positive contributions; a few are now among the company's stars. Even most of these, however, had to go through a difficult period of adjustment before finding their way to the Dynamic Organization.

The experience of one current senior sales executive is typical of this group. A successful veteran of several wireless companies, he was a prized hire to run an established market, where he butted heads with the culture for a year, frustrated that his knowledge and experience and track record did not seem to count for much at U.S. Cellular. The organization, meanwhile, saw him as more concerned about his own reputation than about his customers and associates. He was on the brink of failure when some very tough love from his own leader forced a gut-wrenching self-examination. He emerged from this crisis, by all accounts, a genuinely changed person, and within a year had turned his under-achieving market into a top performer. He has gone on since then to become a "go-to" leader, a problem-solver who has cracked some of the company's toughest cases.

Some version of his experience—the new leader forced to come to terms with the fact that all his/her prior assumptions about leadership, results, and the relationship between them require radical re-assessment—can be seen in most of those who have made a successful transition to U.S. Cellular. The details vary, but the outcomes are similar: respect for the validity of the business model, the realization that unsung little U.S. Cellular is on to something valuable that has eluded some of the most reputable companies on the planet, and a degree of personal humility in the face of these discoveries.

There is no doubt that the many leaders who failed to make this journey hurt the company, holding back the culture, impeding the performance of their teams, and confusing an organization with mixed messages about leadership. This experience, however, was probably a necessary one in the evolution of the Dynamic Organization, teaching the company some of the critical lessons that helped make possible its subsequent growth.

The most important of these was that culture change is a complex, ongoing, continuous process in which different parts of the organization have different needs at different times. There had been a tendency to think that change was linear, a sequential process that began with Rooney's arrival at U.S. Cellular, continued through the early growing pains, and was progressing toward a (probably) successful conclusion. The painful experience of these new leaders was a reminder that a diminishing percentage of the company had witnessed the entire history of the Dynamic Organization. Each year many people at all levels were joining the story in progress, unaware of the lessons learned last year, or the year before.

The company began to realize how essential it was to help these late arrivals understand what they had missed. Without that critical information, they would make up their own versions of history, shaped inevitably by the baggage they brought with their previous experience. U.S. Cellular would have to provide those missing chapters, or risk losing control of its own story.

The training team had by then developed a number of leadership development programs that were earning rave reviews from participants eager to understand the mysteries of the Dynamic Organization. The problem was that, with demand at that point far exceeding the supply of trainers, new leaders often had to wait a year or more before attending the first of these programs—plenty of time for an unsuspecting newcomer to blunder into serious trouble.

The solution was a concerted effort to put a much higher priority on new leader orientation and training. There is always at U.S. Cellular a delicate balance between needs and resources, but the training group found a way to deliver its programs in a timelier and more systematic way, a decision that earned it the gratitude of hundreds of new leaders. These programs have helped address the maddening inconsistency among leaders that had plagued the early development of the Dynamic Organization.

U.S. Cellular was also learning that the D.O. was not for everyone. It requires a unique blend of personal qualities and professional capacity in its leaders, a combination that could not be taken for granted. In the past, the company had been unable to resist a good-looking resume, but it increasingly understood that it had to be much more selective. Associates used the Culture Survey to remind the organization of the damage done by poor leaders. They said, over and over, that they would rather endure an open leadership position for as long as it took to find a good fit for the culture than to live with the pain and confusion of an inappropriate hire.

Eventually, there was almost universal agreement with this proposition. Unfortunately, this had the effect of perpetuating the company's leadership staffing problems. Every market launch or acquisition or internal reorganization increased the demand for effective leadership, while the external supply remained distressingly elusive. The company did not finally crack the recruiting code until 2008. Until then, it would have to wait until it could develop a more reliable internal stream.

Each year many people were joining the story in progress, unaware of the lessons learned last year, or the year before. The company began to realize how essential it was to help these late arrivals understand what they had missed.

Among all the mistakes and wrong turns, a number of very strong contributors did join the company during those years. These successes were more often than not recruited (and then mentored) by the "Lone Rangers," the leaders who had emerged as early champions of the Dynamic Organization and were now moving into more senior positions.

When one of these good fits did click with the culture, that success occasionally opened the door to a succession of good hires, as the recruit told like-minded former colleagues about this amazing organization that actually tries to live its values. Sprint's network department, for example, proved to be a rich vein of recruits, eventually yielding half a dozen leaders whose potential has blossomed in the Dynamic Organization.

These successful recruiting experiences taught the company that there were many wonderful leaders out there in the wide world, gifted people who would thrive in the D.O. if they only knew such a thing existed. They were often frustrated in their current jobs, where their best qualities were usually unappreciated and often unwelcome. To find them, U.S. Cellular would have to start telling its story, letting the world know that there was at least one place that marched to the beat of a different drummer.

All these experiences, good and bad, were deepening the company's conviction that Rooney's business model had it right. Effective leadership is the key variable in business results, the engine that drives the whole enterprise. Just as fundamental was the realization that effective leadership is a scarce commodity in the business world, hard to find and slow to develop. There is never enough of it, and no easy way to increase the supply. A growing company would always need to bring in leaders from outside, but U.S. Cellular would no longer be as desperate, and as undiscerning, as it had once been. The coming of age of a new wave of leaders who had grown up with the Dynamic Organization and understood its demands would mark the first signs of genuine breakthrough.

PHASE 4: THE EMERGENCE OF HOMEGROWN LEADERS

During its formative years, the Dynamic Organization relied more on good luck than good management for the precious supply of effective leadership on which it depended. The emergence of "heroes" like Wright and Hust and Catani had seemed like minor miracles, accidents of time, space, and character that the company could only hope would keep recurring in sufficient numbers to support its growth. While their success had helped to clarify the qualities that constituted the "right stuff" for the D.O., U.S. Cellular had not in those first years been able to reproduce these characteristics deliberately and predictably.

Even during the "breakthrough" year of 2004, the Culture Survey results still indicated a kind of tentativeness around the topic, as leaders experimented with a variety of approaches to make the Business Model work. Some parts of the company, for example, reacted to intensifying competition by making "accountability" their watchword. "Accountability" quickly turned into a euphemism for "make your numbers no matter what." The predictable result was an upsurge in a pounding, intimidating leadership style in which the "how" was overwhelmed by a relentless focus on a numerical "what."

Other leaders became obsessed with the need for greater consistency as the company expanded, leading them to rely increasingly on rules and regulations to produce conformity and generating the first accusations that the inspirational core of the Dynamic Organization was becoming obscured by bureaucracy.

More interesting than these varieties of leadership style was the negative consensus that had developed around them. If some leaders were still struggling to find the sweet spot between associate satisfaction and business results, their associates were becoming increasingly discerning consumers of leadership.

They did not hesitate to point out the gaps they experienced between the theory of the D.O. and its practice. At the same time, they provided hundreds of examples of leaders who clearly "got" the D.O.; their stories gradually became a catalog of leadership behaviors that could be studied and emulated.

A classic example came from a group of veteran network technicians who had for years been adamant in their resistance to change in any form, not to mention the senior leaders who sponsored it. Their stubbornness was reaching the point where a showdown seemed inevitable when a new leader—Kevin Lowell, the first of the Sprint refugees, and now a Network Operations executive—took them on. His approach was to engage them in respectful dialog, listening to their perspective, acknowledging their point of view, while at the same time demonstrating to them how personally rewarding working within this new culture could be.

Later that year, on the 2004 survey, one of these associates announced their capitulation by including a long anecdote among his written comments. Lowell, three levels higher in the chain of command, had asked the team what he could do to help them. This associate responded that, if he was serious, he could "spend a day in my shoes," seeing what it was like to be responsible for so many cell towers covering such a huge geographic area. To the associate's shock, Lowell's response was to ask when and where they should meet. They started at 6 A.M. at the local airport, and eleven hours later they were still driving, and talking.

Stories like these were having as much impact on leaders as on associates. More and more each year were coming to the realization that the D.O. had to be felt, experienced, *lived.*

It could not be reduced to a formula; you just had to *do* it. What's more, the resulting changes might not be limited to the work environment. Becoming an effective D.O. leader could change your life, change not just the kind of leader you were, but the kind of person.

If that was true, it is no wonder that U.S. Cellular was having so little luck in controlling the supply of this new breed. The company could set the goal, describe the requirements, provide information and training, create the conditions for leadership to flourish, but in the end, the decision to be such a leader, the commitment to make the necessary internal changes, could come only from within each individual, one at a time.

If some leaders were still struggling to find the sweet spot between associate satisfaction and business results, their associates were becoming increasingly discerning consumers of leadership.

Second Generation Heroes

The year 2004 marked the point where the Dynamic Organization finally gained traction. Of all the contributing factors to this milestone, none was more influential than the emergence of a group of young leaders who had made their own personal commitment to the culture. Each of them had been present at the D.O.'s creation as associates or supervisors, had become steeped in its values and committed to the business model, had learned from both the early "heroes" and the misfits, and were now ready to share the prime-time stage.

Denise Hutton was one of the most visible of this new

breed. In 2001, she had accompanied Kathy Hust westward to Oregon from Wisconsin, where she had been a store manager. After helping Hust turn the Oregon/California market into one of the first showcases for the D.O., Hutton was the logical candidate to succeed her as director of sales, except for the fact that she was just 23 years old. Knowing how hungry the company was for home-grown leadership, Rooney swallowed any misgivings he may have had and gave her the job. Hutton rewarded his confidence by continuing her market's dominance at the top of the sales and culture survey charts for the next several years. In 2005 she was made responsible for the company's major new market launch in St. Louis.

Michelle Groves was a mid-level manager in the bogged-down Iowa market in 2001 when the dramatic events in Oregon and East North Carolina were signaling a new day at U.S. Cellular. She viewed those pioneer achievements with a mixture of admiration and self-reproach, wondering why she had not been ready to take a similar risk. Determined not to miss another opportunity, Groves transformed herself into a model D.O. leader and a driving force in Iowa's awakening from years of lost potential. Two years later, the difficult Mid-Atlantic market, encompassing huge swaths of Virginia and West Virginia, experienced a spectacular slow-motion leadership wipe-out, with no internal candidates for succession. Few volunteers were eager to relocate to Roanoke for the pleasure of rebuilding a broken and demoralized team. Groves saw the situation differently, as a replay of the Oregon opportunity, and this time she was ready. Her leadership calmed that troubled market and converted it from problem-child into perennial winner.

Chris Rathsack first came to the company's attention as a Wisconsin assistant store manager, when his associates made him one of the first individual leaders to attain a perfect 4.0 on the leadership section of the Culture Survey. He followed that up with similar accolades through a succession of promotions, including a stint as the liberator of north-east Wisconsin from an old-school tyrant who had kept the area firmly under his thumb (and out of the D.O.) for years.

By early 2006, Rathsack was ready to direct a market, and Missouri was badly in need of direction. It had suffered from at least two different kinds of mismanagement since Rooney's arrival: non-benign neglect from a long-time incumbent who found the concept of travel incomprehensible, and good intentions untarnished by execution of any kind from another bewildered AT&T grad. Rathsack represents the D.O. in as concentrated a form as it comes, and the contrast between him and his predecessors bewildered even the show-me state for at least six months. He transformed the market, putting it firmly on the road to company leadership, and in the process was recognized once again as a 4.0 leader. At the 2007 Leadership Forum, nearly every member of his Missouri leadership team joined him on stage to receive Coach Awards. One of them paid tribute to Rathsack's own coaching ability: "You think you're having an ordinary conversation, and after about five minutes you realize you should have been taking notes."

U.S. Cellular's Customer Care Centers seemed to struggle even more than the rest of the company with finding the right leadership balance between the heavy-handed, employees-as-numbers approach traditional to call centers and the excessively associate-centered style of the early D.O. that opened the doors to an infestation of associate entitlement. One of the few care center leaders to master that balance was Nancy Fratzke, who emerged from the Knoxville center to direct its Tulsa counterpart. Her heroic turnaround of that troubled center is recounted in detail in a later chapter.

Engineering had been a sleeping giant for the first few years of the Dynamic Organization, trying at first to resist change altogether and then, under new leadership, frantically scrambling to catch up to the rest of the company. Once its attention was engaged, however, it soon became clear that this workforce of a thousand or so associates who analyzed and solved problems for a living would have a lot to say about the implementation of the D.O. From this group, a small vanguard of leaders began to emerge: people like Lowell, Kevin McNeary in New England, Robert Jakubek in Wisconsin, and Ken Borner in Chicago. They represented an entirely different breed of Engineering leader than the crusty, military-model bosses of the past: thoughtful, curious, intrigued by the potential of this dramatically different approach to getting things done. They became students of the D.O., revealing in the process personal gifts for leadership that had lain dormant under the old regime.

Leaders like these formed a critically important bridge between the handful of first generation "Lone Rangers" and the leadership factory that U.S. Cellular was soon to become. There were still too few of them to meet the demand, but they were living proof that the company was capable of generating on its own the kind of leaders the culture required, without having to depend on external help, either miraculous or conventional.

In fact, it soon became evident that home-grown leaders like these could be even better than the imported variety. Not only did they have a more thorough grasp of the culture as a result of having experienced its formative years, they also had the grass-roots credibility that came from having risen through the ranks. Familiarity was a two-way advantage. The

It soon became evident that home-grown leaders could be even better than the imported variety.

leaders knew all the arcane ins-and-outs of U.S. Cellular's systems and processes and procedures, written and unwritten; and their associates knew them, having worked with them as peers. There was no magic involved. These leaders were "one of us," whose transformation had taken place in plain sight using standard materials available to all: the inspiration of leaders like Rooney and the "Lone Rangers," continual feedback from the Culture Survey, the portfolio of company-developed training programs. If they could do it, so could others.

Beyond their inspirational value, this second generation of leaders lent a more practical hand to leadership development. They formed a core of the company's best talent-spotters, coaches, developers, and role models. Under their tutelage, many associates who had never thought about leadership were now inspired to turn in that direction.

Critical Mass

In 2005, the Culture Survey results surged dramatically, and the Dynamic Organization finally, unquestionably, irrefutably achieved critical mass in a company-wide fusion of the "what" and the "how."

The survey interviews and written comments gave all the credit to a new wave of leadership that was sweeping across the organization. Hundreds of participants praised "the best leader I've ever had" and catalogued the reasons why—an outpouring that has grown louder and longer with each subsequent survey.

Leaders themselves talked eagerly about their personal journeys, often using remarkably similar terms. They had finally realized that the D.O. was important, that it was different, and that, if they were going to be a part of it, they would have to change—not just superficially, in how they approached their work, but within themselves. They understood now that lip service to the culture was not enough. They would have to dig deeper and really begin to live it. One of these leaders offered a typical confession: "I was part-timing the D.O. Now it's full-time, a real embrace. All the values, all the time."

The result of this collective self-discovery was a quantum leap in the number of strong leaders across the company. If the first generation of home-grown leaders developed sporadically and the second took years to emerge, this third generation of D.O. leadership came of age almost overnight, like a pond full of spring peepers that is suddenly, overwhelmingly, *there.*

With numbers came the long-missing consistency. In the past, associates had often pointed out the hit-or-miss quality of leadership, and the two steps forward, step-and-a-half back nature of cultural progress that came with it. Not only that, but the effectiveness of the good leaders was severely diluted when they reported to someone who was still operating on a lower level, or who just didn't get it. The "weakest link" could retard the growth of an entire leadership chain. By 2005, though, it was not uncommon to see reporting ladders that were strong from top to bottom, with effective leaders reinforcing one another at every rung. Associates were noticeably less panicked when an admired leader moved on to the next assignment. They were starting to develop some confidence that the replacement would be carrying the same torch, instead of representing a complete start-over.

With this kind of critical mass came a new awareness of just how unique the practice of leadership at U.S. Cellular was. By definition, an effective leader within the Dynamic Organization exemplified the values and demonstrated the behaviors. But beyond even customer focus and respect and ethics and empowerment and all the rest, two additional characteristics were beginning to stand out, each of which stretched conventional definitions of leadership.

One of these was the quality of caring. An associate wrote, on the 2005 Culture Survey, that "I have lifelong friends who are not as caring and supportive as my leaders." Caring—about customers, about the company, and most of all about associates—had by then become such a defining feature of U.S. Cellular's leaders that the opposite qualities, indifference and/or self-centeredness, were considered infallibly accurate predictors of failure. Leadership in the D.O. goes beyond self, and it does so genuinely, passionately. That passionate tone is set by Rooney himself, who has publicly and repeatedly demonstrated every human emotion on behalf of the customers and associates about whom he cares so much.

Outside observers were noticing this too. Rooney gathers his team on an executive retreat in January, to plan and to begin work on the new year's Talent Review. Each year he invites a speaker to throw light on some aspect of the culture. His guest in 2005 was Jim Kouzes, a researcher and Tom Peters colleague. Kouzes tracks leadership practices, and before he spoke to the U.S. Cellular team, he had each executive complete his standard questionnaire on the characteristics of a leader. He told the group that he was surprised by the results. Usually, he said, the same qualities emerge again and again, in company after company. U.S. Cellular was the only firm he had ever studied where "caring" emerged near the top of the list.

An even more striking presence in the U.S. Cellular leadership mix is the quality of humility. With few exceptions, its best leaders are genuinely humble people. The customer is so unquestionably number one at U.S. Cellular that there is no room left for the kind of personal calculation or "look at me" grandstanding that is taken for granted almost anywhere else.

By 2005, it was not uncommon to see reporting ladders that were strong from top to bottom, with effective leaders reinforcing one another at every rung.

A humble organization has little room for the jousting of egos known euphemistically as corporate politics. We know of no other organization with so many inept politicians in senior positions—one of the highest compliments we can bestow. Some of U.S. Cellular's most powerful executives are almost comically naïve, at least by the standards of most companies. But the values of the D.O. protect any leader who is willing to put all his/her energy into solving customer issues or creating a safe and rewarding environment for associates. On the Culture Survey, one of the words that participants can choose to describe the company is "political." It is typically selected by less than one percent of the population.

"I have lifelong friends who are not as caring and supportive as my leaders."

—2005 Culture Survey Respondent

More than anything else, what differentiates leadership at U.S. Cellular is the paradox that lies at the heart of Rooney's simple-looking Business Model: that superior business results, the ultimate purpose of U.S. Cellular as much as any other capitalist entity, are best achieved indirectly, through effective leadership, associate commitment, and customer satisfaction—always in that order.

Every instinct of any leader schooled in conventional business wisdom drives to the end result. If we want business results, we go get them, taking no prisoners on the way. Rooney's Business Model says: "Not so fast. Build the foundation first, make all the necessary connections, and it will come." It is not easy teaching a mostly young, highly competitive, unquestionably underdog organization to hold its horses, but finally, after five years of patient schooling, that counterintuitive lesson sunk in. The role of the leader at U.S. Cellular is not to pound away at the numbers. It is to build a customer-centered culture that produces numbers as naturally and unselfconsciously as Niagara Falls generates power.

After years of gradually internalizing this Business Model,

WHAT CARING LEADERSHIP LOOKS LIKE

- Lamart Clay was a district manager in Chicago when one of his managers won the coveted Coach Award at the 2007 Leadership Forum. Clay took the time to write a personal note to the manager's father, telling him how proud he could be of his son, then hand-delivered it to the father where he works.

- Shanel Smith was an up-and-coming Chicago store manager who had just been assigned to a new location when she won a Role Model Award for her work at her previous store. She decided to give the trophy to her new team, telling them she wouldn't feel right about accepting it until they decided she should have it. Six weeks later, they presented it back to her.

- Ed Perez's first love is the regional sales organization, where he has been a senior director for many years. He answered a call to join the RSO Marketing Department, however, to help teach that group what the D.O. looked like from a field perspective. This would be his fourth move for the company. He was doing his job admirably in the Product Group when the Brand Group found itself without a leader, just as U. S. Cellular's new branding strategy was about to launch. Perez took on a second job, and the months of 15-hour days that went with it. Later that year his team thanked him the company's highest leader honor: a Coach Award.

- When an associate challenged him to "spend a day in my shoes" to see what it was like to be responsible for cell towers covering a huge geographical area, Network Operations executive Kevin Lowell hopped a plane to do just that.

- Kim Sebastian, a young area sales manager from Oklahoma, did a wonderful job of soothing a troubled Washington/Oregon market as its interim director. When she was offered the position permanently, she had to decline, because she was caring for her ailing parents in Oklahoma. She changed her mind when she couldn't get the words of one of her Washington associates out of her mind: "The D.O. is dead here." She pulled up her roots and went west, living out of a motel for months until the culture was out of danger.

something clicked inside an impressive number of leaders. One participant in the 2006 survey described the process graphically: "It was like hitting a light switch for me. I needed to change my approach, and I can point to a date when I realized that. Business results and morale both increased from then on. It's very powerful to experience something like that."

Experiencing the truth of what Rooney and his executive team had been preaching all these years had a powerful impact on the organization, which was expressed, in part, in a series of overwhelming votes of confidence in the company's senior leaders. By the 2006 Culture Survey, 94 percent of the participants could agree with the statement "I have confidence in senior leaders." Added one respondent: "I'd trust them with my children."

LEGENDS

All strong cultures have legends to support them, stories people tell about their company to help newcomers and veterans alike understand what makes it tick. A good legend becomes a kind of shorthand that explains at a glance how the organization does things.

The first Dynamic Organization legend began at the end of the 2005 Leadership Forum, when Rooney approached the stage to thank his team for finally bringing the culture to fruition. The huge room was momentarily shocked to see tears of happiness streaming down his face. Then they collectively realized how perfectly in character this was. The man's passion—for the company, and for them—was on display, undisguised and unashamed.

A year later, the same thing happened, but for the opposite

reason. The survey results had slipped, and the precariousness of any culture had revealed itself as a threat to the Dynamic Organization. Rooney could have been angry. There were plenty of candidates for blame. Instead, he wept, and everyone present quietly vowed "never to let Jack down like this again." Nothing is more essential to the emerging lore of the D.O. than these two episodes. This culture, people tell newcomers, is not about what you know, or even what you can do; it's about what's in your heart.

An equally powerful legend developed around Rooney's reaction to the company's botched introduction in early 2006 of the federally-mandated emergency 911 program. A key feature of this program was the replacement of older phones that were incapable of making 911 calls. In the last-minute rush to get the system implemented, a well-intentioned but poorly-written letter was released to a number of customers, who interpreted it as an ultimatum. The letter attracted negative media attention, which in turn provoked the interest of a couple of state regulators. To make matters worse, when customers showed up, as directed, to U.S. Cellular retail stores to exchange their phones, an inventory snafu left associates in many locations unable to meet their requests.

A conciliatory letter and great deals in stores for those who had to exchange their phones soon made things right with customers, while the additional store traffic that resulted assuaged the sales associates who had borne the brunt of the initial nega-

> *This culture, people tell newcomers, is not about what you know, or even what you can do. It's about what's in your heart.*

tive reaction. Before long, the incident had blown over. What remained memorable long after the details of the fiasco were forgotten, however, was the open conference call held at the height of the storm to outline the company's response. Rooney came on the call unexpectedly, and instantly defused what could have become an ugly exercise in finger-pointing by insisting that he was personally responsible for the fiasco and that any blame involved belonged to him. Most of the call participants knew that this was not literally true, but they immediately understood Rooney's larger point: that their energies needed to be returned to helping customers, not finding scapegoats.

In that year's Culture Survey, conducted several months later, focus group participants were still talking about the profound impact Rooney's intervention had. By refocusing the company on the customer, he brought a potentially disruptive situation to a satisfactory outcome, and he did so by standing up and taking personal responsibility. Much of the organization agreed with the sales associate who called this "the coolest leadership thing I've ever seen." Another participant's reaction was a little more eloquent: "I've never been more proud to work for U.S. Cellular than I was when listening to Jack's response to the E-911 situation. The tenor of his voice when he said, 'This is not how we treat our customers' is something I think about often. It is the shining moment of my ten-year employment with this company."

Rooney's closing challenge to the triumphal 2007 Leadership Forum is further legend material. After watching six hours' worth of evidence that his young leaders had broken barriers all over the company, his reaction was to raise the bar another notch. Why not, he asked, go for perfection: the ideal associate experience to match the long-targeted ideal customer experience? After all, associate satisfaction was as important a link in the Business Model as customer satisfaction. Why should associates expect any less from their leaders than customers were being encouraged to expect from associates?

And what happened next? Almost everyone took notes and went to work.

We got a phone call late one night from a new Engineering manager in one of the company's midwestern outposts. He had decided that if he was going to live up to Rooney's high expectations, he needed to talk to every leader, from all parts of the company, who had already reached that level of performance. He had already completed his interviews, and he was ready to present his findings and make a personal commitment to his team, but he wanted to check with us first to make sure he had not overlooked anything important. Things like this happen at U.S. Cellular all the time.

Nearly nine years into its obsession with leadership, U.S. Cellular has achieved something remarkable. It has developed a corps of very young leaders, most of them between 25 and 35 years old, who have already learned what leadership is and how to apply it to make things work. It has made its associates experts on leadership, practiced observers of how different leaders meet their challenges, seasoned assessors of what works and what does not. Listen to one of these associates explain her 2007 survey responses: "I scored everything very high this year. It may appear that I didn't put much thought into these topics, but I assure you that I did. I am very appreciative of my leaders and learn something new nearly every day by watching their examples." This is leadership development at its most granular.

The most important outcome of this achievement is U.S. Cellular's enhanced ability to get things done. When it was developing its reputation as the "little engine that could," it reached its goals mainly through sheer determination and hard work. The Business Model was in those early years far from a smooth-running machine, with elbow grease and a lot of improvisation making up for the absence of a steady supply of effective leadership. By 2007, with those gaps filled, the model was operating efficiently, confidence had reached an all-time high, and no problem seemed insoluble. U.S. Cellular's leaders represented a competitive edge that would be virtually impossible, given Rooney's idiosyncratic vision, for competitors to duplicate—and that made its future exciting and full of possibilities.

DO THE RIGHT THING

This has not been a good century, so far, for business ethics. It began with Enron and WorldCom, such profound shocks to the system that many presumed they would be lessons for the ages, chipped-in-stone reminders of the perils—not just to individual miscreants, but to the economy and to society at large—of operating free of ethical constraints. Barely five years later, we find ourselves overwhelmed by the sub-prime mortgage debacle, which seems to have been driven by exactly the same combination of greed and amorality that characterized the earlier scandal. So much for "lessons learned."

So much as well for the clichés about good corporate citizenship that dot the halls and boardrooms, not to mention the annual reports, of any corporation that counts on public favor. Pummeled by a non-stop barrage of evidence that many companies will do anything for a buck—poison our kids with lead paint, our pets with tainted food, our sick with contaminated or useless or downright harmful drugs, just to mention the most egregious examples—is it any wonder that cynicism reigns about "ethics" in business? Who is naïve enough to harbor any remaining illusions that the main motivation of most executives is not their unconscionable levels of compensation? Even *Fortune*, the chronicle of all things corporate, describes this as "the wink-and-a-nod era."

For the idealists among us, one episode among this year's harvest of corporate scandals was particularly poignant. Johnson & Johnson is accused of having "done its best to mislead the F.D.A." (in the words of a *New York Times* editorial) about the safety of a birth control patch it manufactures, increasing the risk of blood clots and strokes in women and prompting more than 3,000 lawsuits. This is the company that, for the past quarter-century, has been the gold standard for corporate conscience, based on its unhesitating willingness to recall another of its products, Tylenol, after some madman had killed seven people by tampering with it after it had reached store shelves. The cost of the recall exceeded $100 million, but the prompt action saved the brand, and added immeasurable value to J&J's corporate reputation.

That was then. Now, apparently, that iconic company is willing not only to jeopardize that reputation, but the lives of its own customers to preserve its precious share of the market. Whatever the final judgment on this case, it is a dramatic validation of the triumph of the "winning is the only thing" ethos.

As sad as this development is, it is hard to blame J&J. Its competitors seem to be just as single-minded about putting their own self-interest ahead of the public's. Hardly a month goes by that some heretofore highly-touted, massively advertised, and immensely lucrative drug has not been found, oops, to be at best ineffective and maybe even downright harmful. The frequency of these incidents is numbing. It is hard for customers not to conclude that every company is doing the same thing.

Thus bombarded, we resignedly conclude that this is just the way things are, an unavoidable byproduct of a free-market economy. If even a formerly high-minded company like J&J finds it necessary to cheat, how can anyone be expected to buck the tide? "Politics ain't beanbag," a sage once said, and neither is business. Leo Durocher, a miserable soul, was right, apparently: nice guys do finish last.

There are, thankfully, at least a few dissenting voices, and one of them belongs to Jack Rooney. What he has created at U.S. Cellular contradicts the prevailing cynicism in two extraordinarily heartening ways. He has shown, first, that it is indeed possible to build a corporate culture that is grounded on high ethical standards: putting the customer first; telling the truth; demonstrating respect and fair play in all its dealings; and insisting that the "what" and the "how" of doing business are inseparable. And second, the company has proved that adhering to such high standards is not a handicap, but a competitive advantage in a marketplace that is starved for a little basic human decency.

Rooney brought a fundamentally ethical way of seeing things—the product of his upbringing and education—to his role as a CEO. There is an ethical dimension, for him, in any situation. Nothing, not even the most abstract technical or financial matter, is morally neutral. There is always, if you think about it carefully enough, a "right thing to do."

It is this ethical perspective that is responsible for the apparent paradox of an executive who cut his teeth as a financial analyst, controller, and CFO approaching his job so personally. Customers and associates are never generalizations to Rooney. They are always people, individuals doing their best in the face of large, impersonal forces. The decisions that affect them need to take that basic fact into account.

Nowhere is his personal approach more evident than in his relations with his call center associates. Most organizations treat them as interchangeable parts, the ultimate cogs-in-a-wheel. Call centers are designed for efficiency, the service industry equivalent of an assembly line, where every transaction is controlled and measured to the nanosecond, and the people who staff them are commoditized as "butts in chairs." Cost-efficiency is everything. If an outsourced and/or foreign butt is cheaper than a current employee's, that decision makes itself.

Rooney loves his call center reps. The call centers are the first places he goes, and he keeps coming back for more: conducting his free-wheeling Straight Talks, wandering the aisles, connecting on a personal basis, listening to the calls that represent a critical link to his customers. Outsourcing this function—these people—is unthinkable to him: clearly not the right thing to do.

U.S. Cellular call centers are strikingly pleasant places to work: roomy, colorful, open, and much bigger than they need to be. In the interest of efficiency, many call centers have adopted the practice of "hoteling," which maximizes cubicle use, forcing employees to share their space with other shifts, or even to move to a different cubicle each day. Rooney hates the concept because it dehumanizes associates. U.S. Cellular's centers provide individual work-spaces for all associates, who are free to personalize them however they want.

When associates and customers are given a human face, the decisions that affect them have, by definition, an ethical dimension. A layoff, for example, becomes more than a fiscal strategy. It is a life-altering event for the individuals involved. From an ethical perspective, a layoff is rarely "the right thing to do," unless of course it is the only way to prevent even greater harm to a larger number. It is a point of pride, not just for Rooney but for almost everyone at U.S. Cellular that, despite the economic volatility of a decade that has seen two major bubbles burst, the company has never laid off any of its associates.

Given Rooney's outlook on life, ethics would be a core value of the Dynamic Organization apart from any question of its strategic value. There is more to the matter than that, however. Ethics also play an essential role in his business model. That model insists that superior results come from customer satisfaction, and that this satisfaction is the product of the customer's total experience with the company. This definition goes far beyond happiness with a particular product or service. It encompasses all the interactions, every point of contact, between company and customer. It recognizes that the thrill of acquiring a hot new handset will quickly be eclipsed by a sales rep's misleading promise or a customer service associate's evasive response.

The underlying premise of this business model is that customers want, recognize, and appreciate fair, honest, and above-board relationships in which they do not need to be constantly on the defensive to avoid being ripped off. Customers will reward with their loyalty a company that earns their trust.

A corollary to this premise is that the associates in such a company will be much more effective than they would be in a less trusting environment, because they have nothing to hide from their customers. The truth is less stressful than deception, and open relationships are healthier than fraudulent ones.

U.S. Cellular has proven that adhering to high ethical standards is a competitive advantage in a marketplace that is starved for a little basic human decency.

The point of the business model is to make money, not to change the world. It encapsulates Rooney's observations about what works best in a retail/service organization. It is only common sense, he says, for such a company to focus on keeping its customers, instead of "firing" them. This approach just happens—because of the nature of what appeals to customers and what repels them—to require ethical relationships. Even if ethics were not so central to Rooney's own belief system, as a hard-headed businessman he would probably insist on including them in U.S. Cellular's formula for success.

This business model might work very well in the hands of a more calculating leader. There is no doubt, however, that much of the force that drives the model at U.S. Cellular comes from Rooney's passionate personal ownership of these values. Ethics, along with customer focus and respect and pride, are far more than effective tools; they are core components of an integrated belief system, a way of understanding how things work.

Culture is, ultimately, about shared values. It may be Rooney's greatest achievement to have built a company of 8,000 individuals who have all come to share a set of beliefs that is ethical at its core. When any one of them talks about "the right thing to do," the amazing thing is that the whole organization always knows exactly what that means.

PEOPLE BEING PEOPLE

The U.S. Cellular of 2000 was probably no less ethical than any other company of the time. Its owners and executives were upright individuals who were as appalled as anyone by Enron and its ilk, and its associates were a reasonable mirror of the prevailing ethical standards in their communities. From the outside, at least, U.S. Cellular seemed typical of any small company scrambling to keep up with a fast-moving world.

Inside, however, a number of conditions had permitted a kind of ethical free-for-all to develop. One of these was the company's heavy emphasis on its bottom line, which had two unintentional effects. First, it focused attention so intensely on outcomes that the methods it used to achieve them got relatively little scrutiny. If making the numbers occasionally required "selling things that don't work," or touting "digital" service in analog-only areas—well, the consequences were not likely to become a problem until the next quarter.

Secondly, the company was in that era, in the frank description of one of its senior officers at the time, "cheap," paying as little as possible for systems, tools, equipment, and people. On the initial culture survey, pay was a huge issue, even though none of the survey questions addressed that topic. While many sales and service reps and their staff support colleagues were happy enough just to get a toe-hold in an exciting, technology-based industry, they were distinctly unhappy with U.S. Cellular's reluctance to compensate them competitively. One of the most common remarks in focus groups was something along the lines of "I could make more money flipping burgers at Wendy's."

"You can't be proud of a business that isn't ethical."

—Jack Rooney

The company's tight-fistedness was responsible as well for the absence of effective control systems. While there were plenty of rules and regulations, there was virtually no enforcement. It did not take associates long to realize that no one, literally, was minding the store. As one early focus group participant put it, "No one is watching over us. They say they are, but no one ever catches us at anything. They don't pay attention to what we do."

Adding up these two factors—ungenerous pay and the lack of management attention—many associates reached the unsurprising conclusion that they were justified in supplementing their incomes however they could. The predictable result was a wide assortment of garden-variety venality, all of which survey participants were happy to itemize: disappearing inventory; free phones and discounted services for friends and family; extremely imaginative misuse of company time; petty theft and pilfering (no communal refrigerator was safe); inappropriate vendor relationships.

The general aura of laissez-faire enabled an equally long list of non-monetary sins: managers asking call center reps to lie to customers about their availability; malicious gossip; the failure of managers (or the HR department) to back up their supervisors on discipline issues; and favoritism in many forms.

The great majority of U.S. Cellular's pre-2000 employees were good, honest people who were just as appalled with such clearly unethical practices as Rooney was. Even these associates, however, were often forced to play fast and loose with company policy in order to reach an ethically desirable outcome. The rules, in those days, were stacked in favor of the company, not the customer, in spite of the usual customer-centric rhetoric. If an associate wanted to achieve what he or she thought was the right result in a given situation, it was often necessary to bend the rules. "We all have our little tricks for short-cutting policy," explained one associate. "We have to sneak around to do things the best way," added another.

Little wonder, then, that the results of the 2000 Culture Survey showed a distinct ambivalence around ethics. The main survey question probing that value is "People here behave ethically," and while 83 percent of the survey population agreed, most of these hedged their bet by picking the "agree somewhat" response. "Ethical" was one of the options on the list of words they could pick to describe U.S. Cellular; it finished as a distant eleventh choice.

Those results, and the anecdotal data that emerged from the interviews, were a long way from being smoking guns. U.S. Cellular was certainly no Enron-in-the-making. Most companies—we have worked with several of them—would consider results like these cause for celebration: no systemic problems, just a few people being people, nothing that might end up the subject of a nasty headline in the local paper, let alone the *Wall Street Journal.*

To Rooney, however, these numbers were a red flag, a sure sign of trouble for his vision. How could he empower his front line associates to give the customer a great experience if they couldn't be trusted to make good ethical choices? How could they make good choices if the company's own policies seemed to be getting in the way? The U.S. Cellular that would, eight years later, stake its brand on the collective instinct of 8,000 representatives to do the right thing was still far in the future. That journey, like the parallel path toward becoming a leadership factory, took place in stages.

PHASE 1: STOP THE BLEEDING

Rooney's first step was to take the pay issue off the table as an excuse for the "help yourself" philosophy that had crept in to many front-line locations. He raised pay scales throughout the company within six months of his taking office, and he made it clear that U.S. Cellular would at least be competitive in its pay approach. The Dynamic Organization would make some significant demands of its people, and they should be compensated fairly in return—and not just using the internal and external market comparisons so beloved by compensation consultants. "Fair," to Rooney, meant enough to support families with dignity, enough to pay for further education and professional development, enough to keep pace with rising costs and nagging economic concerns. From that first year on, pay has never been raised as a significant concern on the survey, with the exception of an occasional specialized skill "hot spot" that is quickly addressed.

A second excuse for ethical laxity—the company's inattentiveness to what was going on beyond the confines of headquarters—disappeared in even more spectacular fashion. Rooney introduced a whole new personal leadership style, in which leaders were expected to know their territories intimately. An organization that had been suffering from neglect now found itself subject to a full court press, as executives started showing up everywhere and asking questions. While their intent was constructive—to communicate, to educate, to raise the flag of the Dynamic Organization, to offer a new kind of role model—they had an important and long-overdue policing role as well. Shady arrangements that had thrived in the dark now found themselves in the spotlight. Their sponsors joined a growing parade of miscreants who were suddenly leaving U.S. Cellular to "pursue other interests." (So many so-called "POI" announcements circulated through the organization during the next couple of years that one focus group comedian was moved to observe that "this POI outfit sure must have great benefits" to be attracting so many of his ex-colleagues.)

Several incidents during these formative years took on symbolic significance as leaders and associates slowly learned where the new stakes in the ground were located, and just how unmovable they were. The most widespread of these became known as "Nokia-gate." The equipment manufacturer Nokia sponsored a popular annual sales contest, one of dozens of such events intended to motivate the sales force and raise its morale. As with all these contests, there were rules, most of them intended to ensure that prizes were being awarded for actual sales of actual Nokia equipment. In the past, little effort had been expended in enforcing them, and some sales associates had become accustomed to pushing the ethical envelope. In late 2001, though, something triggered an alarm at Nokia, and that company blew the whistle, suggesting that many entrants had gone too far in cutting corners. Hundreds of U.S. Cellular sales reps were implicated.

What did it mean, some associates wondered, to be considered somewhat ethical?

In many companies, this kind of thing would have triggered a slap on the wrist, under the general premise that "This is sales—what do you expect?" In the Dynamic Organization, however, it caused an earthquake. After a wrenchingly detailed investigation, the company fired the worst offenders and disciplined the rest, prompting an initial protest followed by a very public debate about the significance of the offense and the fairness of the response. The aftershock lasted a year or more. Many of those who were disciplined correctly deduced that they had damaged their prospects at U.S. Cellular, and left the company. Others, including many who had not been touched by the scandal, refused to participate in any further sales contests. The majority learned some important lessons: sales at U.S. Cellular is as ethical a pursuit as any other; the new values and behaviors were real, not just words on the wall; in the D.O., actions have consequences.

Another practical lesson on ethics involved the open communications that are as vital to the Dynamic Organization as they are counterintuitive to most American corporations. Genuine openness was clearly going to be a lethal blow to leaders who wanted to operate under Rooney's radar. The Culture Survey and Listen Jack, among other innovations, provided a clear channel from front line associates to senior executives, one that associates were embracing with enthusiasm. This was too much for some leaders, who set about trying to cut off, or at least distort, the communication flow.

Listen Jack seemed the easier target, because it was used by individual associates, one at a time. Some managers were so offended by the concept of their associates going over their heads to the CEO that they tried intimidation to ensure their people would never use that outlet. A couple of associates blew the whistle, and investigations ensued. The episode concluded with a dramatic e-mail from Rooney to the entire company, outlining the reasons for the sudden departure of two managers, and using the occasion to emphasize that tampering with precious lines of communication was a serious violation of the Dynamic Organization's values.

These occasional blow-ups were the most spectacular events in the company's struggle to come to terms with Rooney's expectations around ethics, but the greatest progress in the first few years of the D.O. came quietly, as leaders and associates observed, discussed, and absorbed the new cultural direction. The subject was no longer solely a theoretical one, dusted off for ceremonial occasions or the annual report. It was now firmly on the table, posing practical questions on a daily basis, challenging associates in ways that required each of them to develop a personal response.

PHASE 2: "IS THIS ETHICAL?"

If this higher profile was helping to build a more ethical environment at U.S. Cellular, the evidence on the Culture

Survey was not very persuasive. For four years in a row—
from 2001 to 2004—responses to the "People here behave
ethically" question remained static: about 85 percent
agreeing, with roughly half of these agreeing strongly. Okay
results (little more than 10 percent considered their company
and coworkers unethical) but unenthusiastic. Some impatient
participants were beginning to wonder about the persistence
of this core of skepticism. What did it mean, they asked, to
be considered "somewhat ethical?"

Under this frustratingly unchanging surface, however, a
number of developments were taking place that would eventually pay off in an ethical breakthrough. The most important
of these was the evolution of the company during these years
from a state of well-meaning confusion about ethics to the
sharply-focused clarity that was a prerequisite for understanding and action.

At Rooney's insistence, every Culture Survey focus group
probed participants' perceptions of the ethical standards that
they were experiencing. For several years, these discussions
were often a grab-bag of associate concerns ranging from genuine ethical issues to complaints about life's various unfairnesses,
often buttressed by the wide variety of ethical maxims learned
in home, school, and church. Some participants simply labeled
as "unethical" any behavior with which they happened to disagree. At the same time, as Nokia-gate unfolded, it became
apparent that many people had only an uncertain grasp of the
ethical principles that were important to the Dynamic Organization.

As a response to both these concerns, Rooney finally
decided to define, once and for all, exactly what kinds of

behavior U.S. Cellular considered unethical, and to make sure that every associate knew and understood those boundaries. The result was the company's first Code of Ethics, which was accompanied by a multi-module training program covering the typical ethical dilemmas with which associates might be confronted. Every associate was required to take the program and pass a test on its contents. A second set of training modules was introduced a year later.

These actions removed whatever lingering doubt there might have been about how serious the company was about ethics, and raised awareness higher than ever. A survey participant described the difference in the environment: "The last year has opened a lot of eyes. I would have said 'no problem' a year ago. We think more critically about ethics now. We realize it's a bigger issue than we knew."

Leaders reported that growing numbers of associates were using their ethics training as a basis for thinking critically about work situations with ethical implications. "Associates are asking all the time about 'doing the right thing,'" said one impressed store manager. Another marveled that "You hear people stopping to ask 'Is this ethical?' before doing something they've done a hundred times before." That question—"Is this ethical?"—was on its way to becoming one of the company's basic decision-making tools, on the same shelf as "How does this impact customers?"

This enlarged awareness, as healthy a development as it was for the long run, probably prevented the survey results on the ethics question from improving for several years. Issues that associates had not previously classified as "ethical" now caused them to hesitate before giving their seal of approval.

THE "RIGHT THING" REWARDED

An incident from 2003 captures neatly the company's rising ethical consciousness, together with the dawning realization that doing the right thing might even be good for business. A service representative in one of the call centers was caught making a change in the account of a friend, who happened to be a local public official. The company at that time was bidding for the city's wireless business, a fact that the service rep tried to use to evade disciplinary action. Wouldn't it just be better for all concerned to sweep the problem under the rug? Instead, the company contacted the mayor to explain why it felt compelled to withdraw its bid. At the same time, the offending associate was terminated for violating the new Code of Ethics. The city was so impressed with the company's forthrightness that it insisted on doing business with U.S. Cellular anyway.

The very fact that U.S. Cellular was engaged in one of the most effective consciousness-raising movements in corporate history had raised the ethical bar to unprecedented heights.

As associate awareness of ethics grew, so did their pride in the company. U.S. Cellular had put a very visible stake in the ground, one that clearly differentiated it from much of what was going on in the rest of the business community—and associates loved it. "We stand for the customer and our associates," wrote one survey participant. "It's built into our vision. We're the anti-Enron."

One implication of that vision was fast action on ethical violations, like Nokia-gate. Even when those actions caused shock waves, most associates took pride in the company's willingness to put principle before expediency. "We deal with situations now that we used to look away from, as long as everybody was making their numbers," explained one leader. The organization was learning to embrace a stark new equation: "You're ethical, or you're gone."

While associates and their leaders were re-assessing their own conduct from an ethical perspective, there was one proposition on which they were almost unanimously agreed: that U.S. Cellular itself was beyond reproach. The evident seriousness with which the company had worked the ethics value for the first few years of Rooney's tenure was enough to convince most people of its high-minded motives. "We made ourselves question whether we were ethical," wrote an associate on the 2003 survey. "As a result, that value is truly emerging; we're demonstrating it now." While other companies were still embarrassing themselves almost daily, U.S. Cellular had chosen to take a higher road. An engineer confidently predicted that "one of these days a cell phone company is going to get popped for cooking the books. It won't be us." A year later, a colleague followed up on the same theme: "Everybody else is under investigation. Not us."

By then, one of the staple responses from survey participants whenever the topic of ethics came up was that "this is the most ethical company I've ever worked for." This confidence was starting to go well beyond the belief that their senior executives would never do jail time. It was evolving into a much broader sense of ethical conduct than simply obeying the law. Associates now understood that their company was trying to go further than that, to extend the ethics value into an insistence on "doing the right thing" in any situation. "We're one of the few companies that tries to rectify its mistakes," observed a participant on the 2004 survey. A store manager tried to explain what he was seeing: "It goes beyond the Enron stuff. It's basically respect, an everyday way of dealing with people. It's the next level of ethics."

There was no doubt in anyone's mind who was responsible for this amazing change in their company. Rooney and his senior executive team were themselves becoming a source of pride, a striking contrast with the tarnished image of many corporate leaders. "Our executive team are such straight shooters it's almost laughable," according to a focus group of financial middle managers, whose views were widely shared.

For all this encouraging progress, there were still some good reasons why survey participants retained a degree of ambivalence about the ethical climate. Most of their concerns were about their peers, associates and leaders in whose natures was ingrained the impulse to "get away with whatever they can." The depth of this instinct was illustrated spectacularly when the company introduced ethics training. The program was designed for self-study, each module concluding with a test that had to be completed within a specific time. Some associates found a way to cheat on the ethics tests, an act of nerve so breathtaking that large numbers of their peers were willing to blow the whistle on them.

Most of the tension between "getting away with whatever you can" and toeing the ethical line occurred in the two areas that traditionally used financial incentives to motivate associates: sales and collections. Sales associates were partly compensated through commissions on their sales, and further incented by a quota system that required them to make a minimum number of sales each month. U.S. Cellular's commission arrangements were considerably more humane than at most companies, where a dog-eat-dog mentality on the sales floor was usually seen as desirable. Rooney's salespeople were expected to put the customers' interests before their own and to focus on the total customer experience, rather than making the sale at all costs. Still, many sales reps felt pressured by the system, either to keep their incomes up or to keep their jobs safe, or both. And, as countless survey participants pointed out, when push came to shove, some people inevitably put self-interest over integrity. Just one such "shark" disrupted store harmony, putting other associates on the defensive as they competed for sales on an uneven field.

One solution proposed by some associates was to do away with commissions altogether. If they were the root of the evil, why not just put sales reps on salary and remove temptation? That answer was unacceptable to Rooney. Sales by its very nature was competitive. Monetary incentives, they believed, were an important tool to ensure that sales reps brought to their work the relentless, zealous quality prescribed by the Dynamic Organization. The right answer to this dilemma was, they believed, a commission system tempered by another core value, respect for the associate. For example, during an economic slowdown, when store traffic declined, monthly quotas might be forgiven or suspended. At one point, the company changed the commission plan to try to encourage reps to sell new national plans with bigger monthly rates just as the economy was stumbling. The unintended result was a decline in commissions instead of the expected increase. As soon as Rooney learned (through the Culture Survey) that some associates were suffering as a result of the change, he immediately rescinded the new plan, replacing it with one that would enable the sales force to maintain their incomes.

In return, U.S. Cellular expected its salespeople to demonstrate the moral strength to compete fiercely but ethically, to be accountable for both their results and their behavior. This was a difficult balancing act, and the company was discovering that it required associates and leaders of unusual integrity. Many of its existing sales staff would prove to have that quality, or would show the ability to develop it. Many others, however, never mastered that challenge; their continued presence, as the company gradually winnowed them out of the organization, was one of the main reasons why so many survey participants remained reluctant to say without exception that "people here behave ethically."

> *We think more critically about ethics now; we realize it's a bigger issue than we knew.*
>
> —2003 CULTURE SURVEY RESPONDENT

A similar situation was playing itself out in the company's collections department. This was a new internal function at U.S. Cellular, started by Rooney in 2002, partly in response to the company's growth and partly because of his distaste for outsourcing any part of the customer experience—even when those customers are behind in their payments. Collections is a tough business, and associate incentive plans have often played an important, if controversial, role in motivating collectors. U.S. Cellular learned the hard way the care that needs to go into the design of these plans: generous enough to reward initiative and encourage high performance without tempting associates over an ethical line in dealing with customers. At the same time, it insisted that its collectors bring a level of personal integrity to a role that, in too many organizations, is conducted on a no-holds-barred basis.

Outrage as a Sign of Progress

Associate anger over an incident that occurred early in 2003 demonstrated how seriously they were coming to take real or apparent violations of trust. The issue was the company-wide performance appraisal system, through which every associate was assigned to one of four performance categories. During the first frantic years of change under Rooney, most associates had been working harder than ever before, and to higher standards, putting pressure on the upper two categories ("exceeds expectations" and "far exceeds expectations"). For the previous year or so, associate frustration had been growing at the difficulty of ascending to either of these categories, as the company tried to hold the line against rampant performance (and pay) inflation. By 2003, many were convinced that Human Resources was enforcing a rigid Bell Curve, forcing appraisals into a predetermined distribution that failed to recognize actual contribution. The uproar was so great that a Human Resources executive (since departed) issued a formal denial of the charge. There was no forced distribution system, he said, therefore no performance ratings were being arbitrarily lowered to fit into it. Case closed.

Unfortunately, the statement was false. That same executive had in fact quietly imposed a rating quota system the year before. Regional HR representatives had been insisting all along that local leaders alter their appraisals to conform to it. Instead of admitting the scheme, his denial dragged other executives into the mess.

Bringing it all to a head was an Engineering leader who saw fit to send a broadside e-mail accusing senior leaders of covering up the quota plan. This leader was terminated shortly thereafter for an unrelated reason, but the close connection between his accusation and his departure compounded the damage. By the time Rooney and his team realized all the facts of the case, corrected the misinformation in the earlier denial, and dismantled the illicit system, they were faced with a company-wide furor based on the belief that a leader had knowingly lied, then covered it up by firing a courageous whistleblower. And this from an organization that preaches ethics!

Behaving like an ordinary company had ceased to be an option for U.S. Cellular.

On that year's culture survey, hundreds of participants unburdened themselves with comments about this whole knot of connected issues. The prevailing sentiment was that the terminated leader had done what his ethics training had told him to do—speak up in defense of the truth, even at personal risk—and look what happened! "This was an ethical issue," wrote one typical participant, "and we behaved like an ordinary company."

This painful episode took untold hours of communication, discussion, and clarification before the organization was finally reassured that this was an aberration, and that it could safely trust the word of its most senior leaders. It did represent a milestone, however, in the company's maturation. During the long period of resolution, many leaders and associates came to realize how extraordinary it was that the entire company was engaged on what was fundamentally a question of ethics: a question that would probably not ever have been raised in most organizations, let alone captured the attention of senior leadership for the better part of a year. Behaving like an ordinary company had ceased to be an option for U.S. Cellular.

PHASE 3: BREAKTHROUGH

Five years of effort finally paid off in the watershed Culture Survey of 2005, when the ethics results made the long-awaited breakthrough. Nearly 90 percent of the participants agreed that "people here behave ethically," with, for the first time, a majority of the company (55 percent) agreeing strongly. The second most popular descriptor of U.S. Cellular was "ethical," trailing only "customer focused." These numbers were truly astounding, and they only got better over the next two years. By 2008, the "strongly agree" figure had reached 66%.

Stay with these numbers a moment. U.S. Cellular has become a company in which nearly everyone feels good about the ethical climate in which they work, and where more than sixty percent go even further in their endorsement. This achievement is against the background of whole sectors of the economy plunging into disrepute, primarily because of flawed ethical choices; of compromised moral authority among the nation's leaders, because of their willingness to fudge the truth to achieve their aims; of cheating so rampant in our schools (90 percent of high school students admit to it, according to one recent study) that it is easy to wonder what happened to our collective moral compass.

The contrast between their own experience and what they saw occurring in the larger society sharpened the sense of uniqueness that many U.S. Cellular associates were by now experiencing. "You don't get disappointed around here," was the comment of a technician in 2006. "The company always does the right thing."

Each culture survey was a trove of testimonials to the high road U.S. Cellular had chosen: "With so many Enrons screwing their employees, this place is paradise," according to a 2005 participant. The same year an accountant marveled that senior leaders always seemed to choose "the right thing ahead of the business thing." A sales manager offered that "when something goes wrong, we try to fix it." A customer service rep said that "it makes our jobs easier, knowing we won't ever have to apologize to anyone." In the last chapter, we noted that it was typical, by 2004, to hear survey participants talking about their company as "the most ethical they had ever worked for." After that, the praise level began to escalate, to the point where dozens of comments cited U.S. Cellular as "the most ethical company in America."

Ethical dialog at U.S. Cellular had clearly moved to an even higher plane than it had occupied for the first five years of the Dynamic Organization. There were several reasons why the ethics value flowered so fully at this point.

One was the maturing of the notion that ethics are at bottom an individual matter, not just a company or a senior leader responsibility. The years of training and discussion had brought about a widespread realization that each associate is personally accountable for making ethical choices. Further, there was growing evidence that associates were extending this sense of personal responsibility to include helping their colleagues to make ethical choices as well. In previous years, most associates had been content to describe the ethical climate by using the old formula of "the company's great, just a few individual problems." Now they increasingly saw those few individual problems as a serious challenge for which they shared responsibility.

One manifestation of this healthy development was the company-wide loss of patience with the now-legendary bad apples, the diminishing handful of holdouts who persisted in trying to game the system. At one point, most associates had extended a live-and-let-live tolerance to these people, but those days were over. Now the prevailing sentiment was that "having ethics on a job changes everything." Conversely, "a bad apple ruins your team." Leaders noticed that their teams were starting to step up to take ownership for the culture, calling out any peer behavior that damaged it. "People come forward now. They say 'There's something funky in my store.'"

The same impulse showed up in a growing demand that Human Resources be more aggressive in culling the bad apples. HR tended to be cautious in policing the company's system of progressive discipline, making sure that, unless an outright violation of the Code of Ethics was involved, associates were given every opportunity to get back on board before making the decision to terminate. Now associates were insisting that HR hold people accountable for their compliance with the D.O.'s values and behaviors, not just the letter of the law. "We need to make it easier for those who won't buy in to the D.O. to go away," argued a front-line leader, a view that was echoed across the company.

A second reason for the ethics breakthrough was a corollary of the first: if ethics is ultimately a personal issue for which each individual is responsible, then it is essential that the company recruit and hire people who share that perspective and are capable of putting it into action. It makes sense to "winnow the bad seeds" only if they are replaced by good people with whom the D.O.'s unique demands resonate.

U.S. Cellular had always struggled to recruit top talent. It operated, for the most part, in areas where the labor pool was not particularly deep, and it had never been an especially generous, or attractive, employer. Even after several years of positive change, the company remained a well-kept secret, to the frustration of associates who were increasingly amazed that the world was not beating a path to its door. For virtually the entire history of the Dynamic Organization, one of the company's most galling frustrations was its inability to attract top-drawer talent to its open positions. Leaders were too often put in the position of having to choose between operating shorthanded while holding out for a strong candidate who could succeed in the D.O., or relieving the work pressure by settling for any warm body.

Leaders noticed that their teams were starting to step up to take ownership for the culture, calling out any peer behavior that damaged it.

The company's recruiting challenges were still daunting in 2005, but by then it had at least recognized the importance of finding high quality candidates for every position, no matter how painful it was when key jobs lingered open for weeks and months. Further, "high quality" had to be defined in the unique terms of the D.O. The company had learned the hard way that a conventionally good-looking resume could very well camouflage a disastrous hire.

In response to these lessons, U.S. Cellular had installed an elaborate assessment system designed to ensure that its new hires were good fits for the culture. This system caused more than its share of frustration, as the Human Resources group struggled to cope with heightened administrative responsibilities. For years, the hiring process generated box-loads of teeth-grinding horror stories about good candidates falling through the too-wide cracks in the system. Gradually, however, careful selection began to have an impact. U.S. Cellular developed a reputation as a hard place to get into—but one that was worth the pain for those who were able to endure it.

Beginning in 2005, and increasingly thereafter, survey participants recognized the difference higher standards made. They saw that the company was no longer content to accept the damage done by "just a few bad seeds." Instead, it was now one of the few companies willing to try to eliminate this possibility, by insisting on hiring people with the moral fiber to withstand the temptations of empowerment. The fact that "we hire people with character" was becoming yet another reason to be proud of U.S. Cellular.

The final and most important reason for ethics' soaring status was more complex than any of the others. The whole definition of ethics was evolving in a way that made it far

> *The whole definition of ethics was evolving in a way that made it far more encompassing than the specific list of do's and don'ts that formed the original Code of Ethics.*

more encompassing than the specific list of do's and don'ts that formed the original Code of Ethics. A gradual convergence of the values had been taking place over the years, as leaders saw how intertwined they were in reality. Ethics was not something separate from customer focus, for example; they were actually two aspects of the same set of actions, a propensity to do the right thing in any customer transaction. The identical argument could be made for ethics and respect, except that the net was cast even wider to include associates and leaders as well as customers. Something similar was true of ethics and empowerment: true empowerment meant using one's initiative to ensure the right result for the customer and the company. Ethics and pride were organically connected as well.

The centrality of ethics was made explicit in 2005, when Rooney and his executive team decided to make the first addition to the definition of the Dynamic Organization since its inception more than a dozen years earlier. They added a new value, diversity, as a response to an internal discussion that had been going on for some time. What they meant by diversity was not initially well-defined, and for at least two years the company did not seem to know exactly what it wanted to do with it. But the strongest argument on the subject was the simplest: it was the right thing to do, something that the company could not, no matter what complications might ensue, fail to support.

All these developments had by this time become bundled into an overriding sense that regardless of the situation, U.S. Cellular would always do the right thing, automatically and instinctively. It did not matter what heading the action came under—ethics or customer focus or respect or diversity. Recalling the "philosophical algebra" of Rooney's student days, they all pretty much added up to the same thing.

"We admit our mistakes."

The company itself had become the best role model for demonstrating these converged values in action in a variety of situations. Early in 2005, for example, the payroll team discovered that overtime was being calculated incorrectly, in the company's favor, and that the same mistake had been occurring for the previous three years. No one had complained. The issue could have been swept under a rug, or the correction could have been made on a "from now on" basis. Instead, the company "blew people away" by admitting its error and making the changes retroactive to 2002.

We recounted Rooney's handling of the E-911 problem in early 2006 in a previous chapter, using it to illustrate his concept of leadership. The same incident was also an ethical benchmark for many associates, as the company recovered from a faux pas that had offended some of its oldest customers by admitting its mistake, apologizing profusely, and backing up its words with an extraordinarily generous offer that not only repaired the damage but cemented old friendships.

U.S. Cellular had operated a small, inefficient call center in Medford, Oregon for years, a unit that had been particularly creative in finding ways to distort the D.O. to its own advantage. In the spring of 2005, matters came to a head on what local associates insisted on referring to as Black Friday, when 15 associates were terminated for persistent work avoidance. Most of the center went into mourning for the departed (even as they frankly acknowledged their guilt), and stayed there. A year later, the company closed the center as part of its strategy of consolidating its service footprint around its Midwest core.

The circumstances seemed ripe for a monster public relations fiasco: the greedy, vengeful corporation getting even with an outspoken band of local victims. That is how it might have played out in most companies. Instead, U.S. Cellular offered jobs in its other call centers to any associate who was willing to move, very generous severance and placement assistance to everyone else, and a significant contribution to a local park. Executives, including Rooney, descended on the center to meet with every associate to explain the decision and help them with the transition. What could have been a disaster turned into a gigantic love-in, with a memorable farewell party that included a testimonial by the city to U.S. Cellular's corporate citizenship. The company has, despite the closing, continued its multiple-year reign as Oregon magazine's "best place to work in Oregon."

It is in the genes of most American corporations to hate government regulation, and they hate the requirements of Sarbanes-Oxley, because of their intrusiveness, most of all. Even those who acknowledge the justice of the Enron/World-Com payback consider the measure excessive, the corporate equivalent of the principal making the whole class stay late because a couple of kids acted up. U.S. Cellular's leaders may feel the same way, in their heart of hearts, but you can't tell by their actions, as the long-running Gamma saga demonstrates.

Gamma is a huge, multi-faceted project intended to enable the company to track its far-flung assets, a Sarbanes-Oxley requirement. This was a long-standing weakness of U.S. Cellular going back to the old "command without control" days. Most of its network "maps" existed only in the memories and on the personal spread-sheets of its engineers and technicians. Gamma would finally change all that, but at a huge cost. The new program was unwieldy and inefficient, requiring massive adjustments in how network techs did their jobs. It was a major addition to work loads that were already onerous, and, for the first year or two, did not even work very well. For three consecutive years it was a huge distraction for Network Operations and Engineering associates across the company, and a near-obsessive topic in Culture Survey focus

ETHICS AND PRIDE

U.S. Cellular's high ethical standards are a source of pride for associates. Here is just a small sample of their many Culture Survey comments over the years:

- "One of these days a cell phone company is going to get popped for cooking the books. It won't be us."
- "We're the anti-Enron."
- "Everybody else is under investigation. Not us."
- "Our executive team are such straight shooters it's almost laughable."
- "We're one of the few companies that tries to rectify its mistakes,"
- "It's basically respect, an everyday way of dealing with people. It's the next level of ethics."
- "You don't get disappointed around here. The company always does the right thing."
- "We hire people with character."

groups. Its negative impact on the culture was cited as a significant factor in the decline in results on the 2006 survey.

Typically, the company stuck with Gamma, gradually fixing the bugs and improving the process until, by 2007, its negative impact had diminished to the status of "mild irritation that we can live with." One network tech pronounced an appropriate benediction on the subject by reflecting, when a focus group turned once again to that topic, that "Gamma teaches you patience."

Amazingly, however, as some of the pain of the Gamma experience faded away and associates began to gain perspective, what struck them most was the ethical dimension of the company's commitment. "Gamma is a huge investment in doing the right thing," summarized one survey participant. Most of his colleagues agreed. As much as they may have hated how Gamma changed their jobs, they came to see their company's obsessive right-doing as a source of pride. An engineer captured this sentiment in 2006: "Sometimes we go overboard. Some of what we have to do for accounting is wild, but you can understand it when you see those CEOs on TV marching off to jail."

Nothing demonstrates more clearly how deeply-rooted the instinct to do the right thing has become at U.S. Cellular than the restatement episode. The company's external auditor would not sign off on its 2005 financial statements because of a minor concern about how its real estate leases were being recorded. Resolving the issue forced the company to confront, once again, its historic internal control issues, a process that turned into a series of linked nightmares involving several departments and occupying two years. The longer the situation went on, the wider the ripples it caused. Until 2005 was resolved, no 2006 statements could be issued; executive bonuses were held up; stock options could not be cashed.

While all this was going on, U.S. Cellular was embarrassed to be publicly identified as one of those corporations forced to restate its earnings, a phrase that for most consumers means "caught in the act of defrauding its customers."

What an irony for an organization that had staked its future on customer focus!

Throughout this painful experience, associates never lost confidence in the rectitude of their company or its executives. They were impatient with how long it took to get the issue resolved, fearful about the impact negative publicity might have and hopeful that the problem would lead to long-awaited upgrades in the way the company handled data. They eventually became frustrated with having to defend the company to skeptical friends and neighbors. But they always remained certain that there was no smoking gun to be found anywhere in their organization.

They expressed their confidence on the two Culture Surveys—2006 and 2007—that were conducted during this period. The restatement issue was nothing to be ashamed about; instead, it was evidence of the company's high standards. "We blew the whistle on ourselves," commented one close observer. Another added, "This is so typical of U.S. Cellular—our leaders tied up their own stock to get the records fixed."

The drama finally concluded in early 2008 when all the delayed reports were issued and the key credit agencies gave their blessing by upgrading U.S. Cellular's rating. In the end, what could have been a confidence-breaker had only strengthened associates' conviction that their company was occupying extremely high, and very lonely, ethical ground.

BASIC GOODNESS

The stories associates tell about the basic *goodness* of their company and the people who work there go on and on. The following comments are just a few of the unaided responses that turned up in the 2007 survey write-ins:

- "After the ice storm last year, some associates and their kids were left without heat, so we put them up in hotels. What other company would do that?"
- "We do things on a daily basis that other companies would never do. One of our customers lost her home in a tornado, and my team got phones and chargers to the family and made sure the bill was paid. We never think twice about it."
- "We don't just write checks—we show up with our sleeves rolled up."

Virginia Tech is located in one of U.S. Cellular's markets. As soon as the 2007 shooting tragedy unfolded, engineers installed a temporary cell site on campus to handle the communication overload, providing an essential link in the university's response. In a news conference, the campus police chief publicly thanked the company—although, as luck would have it, he misnamed it "Verizon" in the confusion. Nevertheless, U.S. Cellular won thousands of friends for its instinctive reaction. An associate who spent that week working on campus recalled that "people would come up when I had my logo-wear on and thank us. It brought chills to my spine and tears to my eyes."

When National Guard units began to be called to active duty in Iraq and Afghanistan, Rooney quietly informed the U.S. Cellular employees who were affected that their pay and benefits would be maintained, that their old jobs would be held for them, and that their families' cellular phone charges would be waived until they returned. There was no need for debate or discussion or policy review. It was clearly the right thing—no, the *only* thing—for a values-driven organization to do under the circumstances. Never mind that, as the war has stretched into years and National Guard commitments have extended far beyond anyone's expectations, many employers with outstanding reputations have scandalously reneged on their initial commitments to their soldier/employees.

One day in 2006 a general in the Illinois National Guard happened to be meeting with Jeff Childs, U.S. Cellular's Senior Vice-President for Human Resources, to plan a job fair for returning veterans. Childs mentioned in passing what the company was doing for its Guard members, and the general was nearly floored by its generosity, compared with the attitudes of many of the organizations he was dealing with. He was even more astounded by the company's modesty in offering this extraordinary support entirely outside the spotlight. He insisted on marching next door to Rooney's office to nominate him on the spot for a Patriot Award.

As a totally characteristic footnote to this story, when Rooney received the award, he displayed it proudly in his office, but it never occurred to him to tell anyone about it, until Childs reminded him that his associates would be proud to know what their company was doing to support their troops.

These stories represent the tip of an incredible achievement. At a time when public cynicism about institutions in general and business in particular is limitless, U.S. Cellular has set its ethics bar almost foolishly high—and then exceeded those expectations.

PART 3

Defending the
Dynamic Organization

MOVING
THE BIG ROCKS

One of the pitfalls of history is the sense of inevitability it conveys. Looking back from today's perspective, it often seems that things could only have turned out the way they did. Success stories like this one, especially when condensed to the readable highlights, usually have a quiet beginning, a period of struggle and frustration in the middle, a critical turning point or two, and then a triumphant sweep on to the happy, or at least hopeful, ending. Progress, in retrospect, seems like a straight-line process, with no significant detours and an outcome that was never in serious doubt.

That's not how it happened at U.S. Cellular. As gratifying as the first eight years of the D.O. appear in retrospect, they were marked by problems that at times seemed intractable, and by several serious mis-steps that could easily have derailed the whole experiment. Some of the challenges faced—such as integrating an acquired company into the culture, with the purchase of PrimeCo in 2002—were predictable. Others, like an outbreak of entitlement in the call centers, were unforeseen negative consequences of developments that were positive on the whole. Perhaps the most painful setbacks were the result of outright gaffes.

One of the great strengths of the Dynamic Organization has been the forthrightness with which problems and errors—including those made by senior leadership—are acknowledged. A problem is a problem—and it needs to be fixed, not glossed over or worked around.

And who fixes these problems? There is only one possible answer in the D.O.: effective and courageous leadership fixes problems, just as surely as lazy or careless leadership causes them. Some of the company's greatest success stories started with a leader-made mess or mistake—and ended as testimony to the essential wisdom of the business model.

FROM COWBOYS TO CUSTOMER CHAMPIONS

No group better represented the strengths and weaknesses of pre-2000 U.S. Cellular than its Network Operations/ Engineering department, whose nearly 600 associates formed the core of the company's technological expertise. This was a proud, long-tenured, can-do group, many of whom had quite literally built the company, going back to its very first cell towers in Knoxville, Tennessee, in the late 1980s.

Much of that building had been done on a shoestring, and these technicians were exceptionally proud of their ability to do whatever it took to keep the network running. The department in general, and the network techs in particular, were less a team than a collection of rugged individuals operating with few rules, little supervision, and a lot of ingenuity. They had little contact with their co-workers, and even less with customers. They were the company's cowboys.

That was how department management liked it. The longtime executive in charge was an old-fashioned autocrat who practiced a divide-and-conquer style, pitting units and individuals against one another to keep them off-balance and edgy. Mutual distrust was a departmental hallmark.

Enter Rooney and the Dynamic Organization. While most of the company's other major units received the news hopefully and with a relatively open mind, the reaction of the Network Operations/Engineering group was simply, "Ain't gonna happen." They were not about to change their style to accommodate the new guy's cockamamie notions about culture.

Their defense strategy was a subtle combination of open resistance and passive aggression. The departmental party line was that the D.O. was nothing new, just a warmed-over mix of common-sense clichés that most people learned in childhood. Besides, this department had already been operating that way, but without the fancy name, for years. No change, therefore, would be necessary, thanks very much anyway. To prove this last point, the department manipulated its Culture Survey results so that they were pleasingly robust. As an exclamation mark, one of the most unreconstructed of the executive's cronies and a world-class practitioner of nepotism himself somehow managed to win a leadership award on the 2001 survey, to the bemusement of the rest of the company.

The charade ended the next year, when the department head was finally induced into retirement, quickly followed by the posse of like-minded henchmen that formed the unit's chain of command. Their replacements were a different breed—younger, more attuned to customers, less driven by internal politics and personal power, and secretly curious about the cultural transformation that had bypassed their department. They represented the fertile ground for the Dynamic Organization that Rooney had long sought on the technical side of the business; it seemed quite possible that, at long last, the D.O. might extend its reach across the entire company.

But first there was the unfinished—unstarted, really—business of creating the network of Rooney's vision. That meant more than just being competitive with the so-so standards of the dominant companies in an industry that made few customers happy; it meant introducing the unprecedented levels of wireless reliability and consistency befitting a truly customer-focused organization

There was just one problem: a network as flawless as that would require major changes, not just in equipment and tools, but in many of the attitudes and behaviors at the heart of the department's cowboy culture. A network for the Dynamic Organization meant company-wide standards, consistency of approach, controls, communication, and an end to the traditional free-lancing that had been justified under the banner of empowerment. To many associates, this reasonable-sounding agenda sounded more like a declaration of war.

The department fought back, using every weapon it could think of. It ridiculed the "company-wide consistency" argument. Hadn't the new regime noticed the extreme variations of conditions they dealt with, from the mountain blizzards of the Cascades through the tornado-swept plains of Oklahoma to the coastal hurricanes of the Carolinas? One size could not possibly fit all the situations they dealt with.

That argument was just the starting point. Each new directive produced head-shaking indignation, followed by hand-to-hand combat. A change management system, designed to ensure that an independent-minded tech would not inadvertently bring down the system, brought the unit to the point of rebellion. Another new requirement—that customer-affecting maintenance be done at night instead of whenever it suited the tech—poured more fuel on the fire. For most members of the

Network techs were less a team than a collection of rugged individuals operating with few rules, little supervision, and a lot of ingenuity. They were the company's cowboys.

department, this was too much change, too soon, from too far away. Wasn't this Dynamic Organization supposed to respect associates' opinions too?

The mounting frustration came to a head on the 2002 Culture Survey. An organized write-in campaign catalogued the many sins of the new regime and underscored the department's low morale, which in turn had a depressing effect on the company-wide results. The engineers' public tantrum made it clear that bringing them and their network into the D.O. could well be a difficult and drawn-out process. Something, obviously, had to give.

Neither side conceded an inch for the next few months.

Department leaders offered appropriate words unmatched by any real attempt at reconciliation; associates responded with a campaign of passive resistance. None of the proposed initiatives gained any traction. The extent of the stand-off was evident when, in early 2003, we began a series of mid-year reviews to assess the situation. The point of the mid-year review is to track progress in a troubled unit, on the standard U.S. Cellular assumption that its leaders have been working conscientiously since the prior Culture Survey to address the issues identified. In this case, however, it was immediately obvious that meaningful change was stalled in its tracks.

Our first stop was Morgantown, the pretty gateway to hilly West Virginia, beautifully scenic for most of the year, but an intimidating beast in a snowy January. The mood in the focus group of eight engineers and network techs—about half of that market's complement—matched the weather. The participants were even angrier than they had been six months ago, because, as far as they could see, nothing had changed. No one was paying attention to their concerns. Department leaders were as remote and unyielding as ever; no dialog had been initiated, no explanations offered, no olive branches extended—just more and more top-down directives that failed, as the engineers saw it, to respect who they were and what they had done for the company. Our discussion notes were almost identical to those from the previous summer—a sure sign of big trouble in a company that takes "dynamic" as literally as this one.

We sounded the alert as soon as the interview ended: something dramatic needed to happen, fast, to avert the train-wreck that would surely be the outcome of another dismal survey later that year.

That alarm-bell finally forced the embattled leadership team to confront the unfamiliar behavioral implications of this odd specimen of a culture. With Kruger's help, they approached the problem as an engineering challenge, one that required analysis, diagnosis, and a logical plan—and with the resulting blueprint in hand, they followed the Rooney template and hit the road, taking the case for change directly to their front line teams.

These initial ice-breaking forays evolved into a series of extended tours that went on for years, becoming the department's standard methodology for dealing with conflict. Week after week, leaders met their scattered teams in small groups, painstakingly reviewing plans, explaining strategy, listening to the questions, the concerns, the rants against change.

They found a way to articulate Rooney's technical vision in human terms. What if the network in Oregon needed help from the techs in Iowa or Maine? The company needed to be able to send techs to any market knowing they could do their jobs just as effectively as in their home territory. That was why consistency was important. When they put it in those terms, their listeners grudgingly acknowledged that they just might have a point.

Most of all, the new leadership team got to know who these proudly independent people were and the many worthy things that they had accomplished in the pre-Rooney years; at the same time, associates got to know their leaders as more than cold-blooded technocrats. By the next year's survey, the West Virginia engineers and their peers across the company were eager to tell us about what real people their bosses had turned out to be. Not all of them agreed with every detail of the department's new direction, but they at least understood it, they were talking about it, and many had even come around to support it.

Once this mutual learning process was under way, it proved impossible to stop. A year later, there was near-unanimity on two points: it was a pretty neat company where you could actually have a normal conversation about real life with officers and directors; and those changes they were pushing actually made a lot of sense, when you thought about it.

They did think about it. The conversation begun in that first dreary winter engaged the department, and, as many of them pointed out in survey comments over the next few years, they are engineers, after all. This Dynamic Organization that seemed to be keeping their underdog company in the game when others were laying off their technical people was an interesting subject that merited their attention. Under the tutelage of an expanding cast of bright young leaders, they became students of the D.O., dissecting its tenets and then putting them back together again, often with new ideas for applying them more effectively.

For the next several years, there was no more stimulating place to be than an engineering focus group in West Virginia or New England or St. Louis, listening to the participants argue the finer points of leadership in a technical environment, the impact of corporate ethics on customer satisfaction, or the interplay between pride and empowerment.

Customer focus was an especially intriguing topic. The department had only a tenuous link to customers up until then. Customers were obviously the beneficiaries of their work on the network, and they were no doubt the source of the revenue that kept the company in business and food on their tables. But engineers and technicians rarely came face to face with a customer; their relationship was more theoretical than real. Now that they were giving the subject their full attention, however, the customer connection came to life, as technical teams sought ways to make customer focus as relevant to their work as it was to their colleagues in Sales and Customer Service.

The Culture Survey comments were a good barometer of the sea changes taking place. We started to collect stories by the dozen of knotty customer reception problems solved by engineers taking their test instruments right into the troubled home, or long-standing coverage issues fixed because the network techs, who know every signal-blocking hill and gully of their territories, got involved in locating cell towers. We heard countless anecdotes about the brand-new sense of pride and accomplishment that came from having customers honking their horns in acknowledgment when they saw their U.S. Cellular trucks. One engineer told of rear-ending a car at an intersection. When the victim recognized the logo, her first words were to thank him for the great service. Meanwhile, sales associates couldn't say enough about the support they were suddenly getting from the engineers in their markets. They seemed to be different people now from the remote loners of the past, engaged teammates who couldn't do enough for either their customers or their fellow associates.

> *One engineer told of rear-ending a car at an intersection. When the victim recognized the U.S. Cellular logo, her first words were to thank him for the great service.*

By 2005, the Net Ops/Engineering group was a pillar of the D.O. They had succeeded in building the network that Rooney had dreamed of in 2000, its reliability confirmed by independent drive-testing. That year, the rest of the company was amazed by the revelation, at the annual Kick-Off Meeting, that U.S. Cellular would soon be ranked either first or second in network quality in every one of its markets. Most associates had been unaware that their little company harbored such an ambitious goal.

The department had worked just as hard and thoughtfully on the D.O.'s "soft skill" requirements. Leaders were spending impressive amounts of "windshield time" in their trucks, conducting team meetings, one-on-one interviews, and "just being there." Leadership results were rapidly improving, as whole leadership chains seemed to mature practically overnight. Associates—those former lone wolves who at one time had been indifferent, if not resistant, to leadership—were effusive about the growth of their leaders and the difference that this made to their teams. By 2007, the department had no weak links in its leadership line-up, and some of the company's brightest future stars.

That year, the depth of this team's commitment to the culture could be seen in the survey data, the best and most consistent in the company. Their achievement was capped by the reaction of the audience at the 2007 Leadership Forum, when Rooney presented a special award for Dynamic Leadership to the entire department, the first time that had ever happened. The meeting erupted in an extended standing ovation, in the same room where such a discouraging verdict had been delivered five years before—final proof that Network Operations/

Engineering was not only "on board," as Rooney had asked, but generating much of the energy needed to keep the culture driving forward.

HR: FROM PROBLEM TO SOLUTION

The Human Resources Department usually gets no respect. HR is much maligned in most organizations as a bureaucratic enclave, and that reputation is often deserved. But it also controls the critical pieces of infrastructure that help drive organizational behavior—recruiting, rewards, recognition, promotions, learning, development, communication—and it makes all the difference in any change process whether these are aligned with the desired outcome or not.

During the first few years of the Dynamic Organization, U.S. Cellular's HR department was so much a part of the problem that it was unable even to identify, much less implement, the solutions that would have accelerated a cultural breakthrough. The department's erratic leadership in the early days made it a dispirited, fearful place, one of the least hospitable environments for the D.O. Instead of modeling the new culture, HR had degenerated into habits of self-protecting political warfare and internal sniping that disqualified it from its natural leadership role.

Its internal dysfunction rendered the department unable to cope with the challenge of reshaping the programs and processes it controlled to help drive the culture. As a direct result of this failure, the company spun its wheels at every rough patch on the journey, forced to substitute hard work and sheer determination for the well-oiled process machinery that could have eased its passage.

The toxic cloud of fear and acrimony that surrounded the department began to lift when its leader—a volatile veteran whose over-the-top explosiveness was the main ingredient in the bad chemistry—finally put himself in a terminally untenable position. His resignation allowed a team that had not realized how tense it had become to start breathing again. Relief at his departure was compounded by the arrival of his replacement, Jeff Childs, a respected professional with a background in sales and marketing as well as HR, who had most recently been running the Ameritech Institute (for leadership development).

Childs was the perfect antidote: smart, strategic, operations-savvy, and totally unflappable. Even more important was his natural affinity for the D.O.'s essential "how." He soon proved to be, in one of the most visible positions in the company, an outstanding role model and coach. He quickly won the confidence of his beleaguered department, and started the long process of gradually turning it into both an advocate and a tool-kit for the D.O. He became the go-to person for any issue requiring a deft cultural touch. His presence brought the executive team together, triggering a surge in the organization's confidence in their senior leadership.

Childs' instant personal credibility with his fellow officers opened doors around the company that had previously been closed to his department. Most leaders had come to view HR with suspicion, believing it more likely to throw gasoline on an organizational fire than to put it out. Now, they were willing to give a second chance to the new generation of professionals Childs had quickly recruited to upgrade his team. For the first time, U.S. Cellular could get trustworthy, in-house, state-of-the-art advice on its training or associate relations or compensation problems.

With the makings of a credible team in place, Childs began a remarkable series of changes designed to transform the department's role within the company. Until his arrival, HR's relationship to the D.O. was as tenuous as any of the staff groups. The new culture was an object of suspicion, as much threat as opportunity. Now Childs charged his directors with taking ownership of the culture. The D.O. was about people and their behavior—home field for any self-respecting HR practitioner. This was—or could be—the opportunity of a professional lifetime, and he expected his team to seize it.

Several changes sought to bring structure, discipline, and accountability to this seismic shift. Regional HR directors, for example, had always reported directly to the senior HR executive instead of to their regional vice presidents—a recipe for political intrigue that kept the regions off-balance. Now these HRDs became part of the regional leadership team, with a direct reporting line to their local vice president. The new arrangement allowed young leaders like Jennifer Hooper to emerge as towers of strength in helping their regional VPs to drive the D.O. It also enabled a number of respected sales leaders to join the HR team—a previously unthinkable development that added further to the department's growing credibility.

To help his new team develop consistency, Childs retained a dotted line relationship with his regional directors. For a time, he had them bring to him any associate relationship issue from anywhere in the company, until they could become comfortable with their roles and consistent in their approach. He continued the department's traditional weekly conference calls, but now, instead of reporting on the latest issues in their functional specialties, he asked his leaders to assess the state of the culture in their areas. Gradually, HR leaders learned the language of cultural accountability.

Other changes followed. HR took strong roles in localized versions of Rooney's Talent Review process that extended its reach all the way to front-line leadership. It centralized myriad scattered local training initiatives into an integrated operation that reflected the D.O.'s core principles, and initiated uniform processes for reading out to their teams the Culture Survey results of individual leaders, and for orienting new leaders to the culture and to their legal responsibilities for HR issues.

This flurry of activity enabled HR to get out of the way, to join the culture, and to become the arsenal of tools and counsel the D.O. needed to thrive. Childs' quiet professionalism made it possible—a fact not lost on observers of the company. Ted Herbert has closely tracked the D.O. from his position as senior HR executive for TDS, the parent company through which the Carlson family exercises its majority ownership of U.S. Cellular. He states unequivocally that "the D.O. got traction as soon as Jeff arrived."

BUT WILL IT PLAY IN CHICAGO?

The biggest and most necessary gamble that U.S. Cellular has taken during the Rooney years—aside from the Dynamic Organization itself—was acquiring PrimeCo in 2002. That struggling carrier had, while undergoing multiple changes of ownership, carved out a small, unsavory niche in Chicago, serving a mainly down-scale market that the national carriers could not be bothered with. Its own associates acknowledged their marginal clientele in the semi-affectionate nickname they had bestowed on their company: CrimeCo. Still, they were a proud band of survivors, a scrappy group that had battled against heavy odds in one of the country's most competitive markets.

None of that mattered to Rooney, except PrimeCo's Chicago franchise. He was eager to get a foothold in U.S. Cellular's home-town for two key reasons. First, for the Dynamic Organization to succeed, he needed to make customers of his executives and headquarters staffers. It would be impossible to ingrain customer focus if none of them carried the company's products in their pockets. Second, Chicago was critical to the reshaped, Midwest-anchored footprint he was building as a more coherent and efficient alternative to the company's old "four corners" map. FCC restrictions on the number of licenses in each market meant that there was only one way for U.S. Cellular to break into Chicago: acquire an existing carrier, only one of which was for sale. From this perspective, the PrimeCo purchase was no decision at all, even though it represented U.S. Cellular's biggest acquisition by far. The company swallowed hard, held its breath, and took the plunge.

PrimeCo was U.S. Cellular's entrée into Chicago, but it also represented a huge barrier to that market as well—an irony that few had foreseen. To be successful, Chicago would have to be a showcase for the Dynamic Organization, a main-stage demonstration that a values-based approach could produce superior results in one of the most competitive arenas in the world. Chicago would be the proof that the D.O. worked in any environment, not just the sheltered conditions of rural America. Chicago would be the flagship for U.S. Cellular, and for its culture.

Unfortunately, there was in the summer of 2002 a vast gap between Rooney's vision and the reality of the company he had bought. PrimeCo's associates were street-smart scrappers engaged with few tools or resources in a kind of urban guerilla warfare, not just with their competitors, but with their own executives and their own equally pugnacious customers. The fine words of the D.O. sounded good to this audience—whatever turned the latest owner's crank—but the hard reality of the wireless business on Chicago's mean streets gave concepts like "ethics" and "empowerment" and "trust" an ethereal quality. They seemed to many of the company's new associates to add up to a recipe for getting yourself hustled.

Bridging a cultural gap this wide would require exceptional leadership, but this was a period in which the company's limited internal pool was already overtaxed just trying to keep up with the transformation that was well under way. All the known "heroes" were otherwise occupied, leaving the task to a checkered succession of leaders whose only consistent quality was an inability to crack the Chicago code.

> *PrimeCo's associates were street-smart scrappers engaged in a kind of urban guerilla warfare, not just with their competitors, but with their own customers.*

It did not help that the market was getting more help than it needed from nearby headquarters. Rooney had wanted his executives to be closer to their customers. Now they were right on top of them, and they made the most of the opportunity. Chicago suddenly had too many bosses, too many ideas, too many back-stairs communication opportunities, and not enough accountability. Empowerment was one early casualty, among many others, as the D.O. floundered.

This was the pattern for the next several years: tremendous activity, lots of hard work, and a major commitment of resources (Comiskey Park, home of the White Sox, became U.S. Cellular Field during this period) adding up to little more than frustration. The only bright spot was the quality of the network, which the engineering team had been polishing to a competitive gleam. It was recognized as the best in Chicago by a local TV network in 2005 and has never relinquished that title.

Through all this, the Chicago market team seemed impervious to the D.O., beyond a superficial appreciation of a much-improved work environment. Chicago customers remained equally indifferent. For several years, business results gained no significant traction. With the whole company anxiously waiting for something to happen, U.S. Cellular's Chicago gamble seemed to be coming up empty.

At the end of 2005, Rooney took his last best shot at quieting the growing band of skeptics who were beginning to suggest that Chicago might be the D.O.'s Waterloo, fatal evidence that his formula would not work in a sharp-elbowed, big city environment. He persuaded one of his most seasoned sales leaders, Don Cochran, to take on the challenge. Cochran had turned the giant Iowa market—second in size only to Wisconsin—from a ragtag operation with a reputation for chewing up leaders into a perennial award-winner on the Culture Survey and a competitive powerhouse. If anyone within the company (and by then Rooney had given up on finding an outside savior) could turn Chicago around, it was clearly Cochran.

Cochran was one of the company's rare external hires to make a successful transition to the D.O., but it had not been easy. He spent a frustrating first year trying to figure out how to apply his exceptional industry knowledge and sales experience within U.S. Cellular's cultural framework, without much success. Suddenly the light went on, and he decided to make an emotional appeal for the hearts of his Iowa team. Borrowing part of the framework of Dr. King's immortal "I have a dream" speech (and agonizing for weeks about whether his intentions would be misinterpreted), he surprised an all-associate meeting with his heartfelt "dream for Iowa," leaving his team in tears with the fervor of his vision. That event marked the beginning of Iowa's rise to dominance, one that witnesses never tired of recalling.

Cochran made a total personal commitment to Chicago, leaving his family in their Iowa home and commuting back there on weekends. He threw himself into the assignment, working at an exhausting pace to lay the foundations for the D.O. in his huge new market. He insisted on taking a disciplined approach to the culture. He made his leaders accountable for conducting regular one-on-ones with their sales reps, installed a system of rotating teams assigned to respond to issues identified in the Culture Survey, and made it a priority to teach every associate the meaning of each value and behavior.

After six months of frenetic activity, however, Chicago was not particularly impressed. Many, in fact, seemed almost offended at the presumption that what worked in Iowa could have the same impact in Chicago. The only values their customers were interested in, they said, were good deals: free phones and low prices. Cool stuff—snazzy hardware and bright colors—was far more important to them than good service. Cochran was certainly a harder worker than any leader they had seen so far, but he was barking up the wrong tree with the D.O.

Bridging a cultural gap this wide required exceptional leadership.

Besides that, he seemed pretty "scary," intimidatingly intense compared to the leaders they were used to, who had made the typical "outsider" mistake of emphasizing pizza and parties on the clueless assumption that this would somehow produce "associate satisfaction." The first survey returns of the new era, in the summer of 2006, were not especially promising. Chicago's results were about where they had been for the previous five years: near the bottom of the pack, and showing no signs of improving any time soon. As for Cochran himself, the verdict was only slightly better. Most of the market did not yet know what to make of him. Whatever farm-belt remedy he was selling, Chicago did not seem to be much interested.

A minority among the Chicago survey participants were beginning to see the light, however. Watching Cochran had helped them put the components of the D.O. together in a way that made sense, even in Chicago. The more they saw him in action, the more they saw that he was no rural yokel out of his depth in the big city. He had a plan for the market, and he was relentless in putting it into action. His personality started to grow on them. Yes, he was over-the-top intense and he could be startlingly direct, but he was wide open and brutally honest, and if he said he intended to do something, you could count on it happening.

Over the next year, Cochran never let up the pace, single-mindedly putting together the team, the structure, and the tools he thought it would take to engineer a Chicago breakthrough. Turnover was heavy. Those who were not willing to help no longer had the option of carping from the sidelines. Open positions stayed that way until a good fit for the culture could be found. Training intensified. A Leadership Academy lit fires under a new generation of young store managers and sales managers. Dozens of new stores opened in more appealing locations. Even the long-slumbering White Sox got into the act. Playing in U.S. Cellular Field, they won the World Series, generating a tsunami of positive publicity and all-around good will for the company.

All these factors were adding up to something big in Chicago. The market's annual dinner meeting for all associates and leaders late in 2006 provided a clue to the magnitude of the change. This had become a formulaic event, traditionally held on a Sunday night after the retail stores closed, centered around a report of the previous year's Culture Survey results, but notable mainly for being sparsely attended and for providing a depressing contrast with the pride and energy on display in other U.S. Cellular markets. Since that year's survey results reflected the usual mediocre showing, there was no reason to expect anything different—especially since the Chicago Bears were playing on Sunday Night Football.

An unsuspecting visitor could feel the energy in the hotel parking lot. Inside, the lobby was jammed with a capacity crowd, whooping and hollering and costumed memorably (Cochran and his leadership team made an unforgettable Kiss). The noise never let up all night, reaching a crescendo when Cochran addressed the crowd.

In the months before the 2007 Culture Survey, isolated rumors about Chicago's awakening were circulating around the company. The market made a monthly budget for the first time ever; it had just passed Wisconsin as the largest market; it was gaining market share from the entrenched competition. The rumors began to concentrate into a buzz that suggested that U.S. Cellular just might have a new sheriff in town.

In that year's focus groups, the market was unrecognizable. Gone was the whining about pay and promotions and all the reasons why failure was inevitable. Instead, we heard a great deal about the affection the participants had developed for Cochran and his team. They knew now how much of his personal life he had sacrificed for their success, how much caring underlay the blunt honesty, how much they had learned, about the D.O. and themselves, without realizing it. Associates acknowledged Cochran's rough edges, but almost invariably concluded their comments with some version of "but I'd follow him anywhere."

The results, by that point, were predictable. Chicago improved more than any other part of the company. It had finally caught up with the rest of the organization, and when it came time to recognize its achievement, the audience responded with one of the day's most prolonged standing ovations. Rooney was not, for a change, the only one crying at that point.

EMPOWERMENT VS. ENTITLEMENT

The front line customer-facing associate is the nuclear heart of every company that provides customer service, but these sales and service providers are traditionally at the low end of the corporate totem pole in terms of working conditions, rewards, and basic respect. This was the core paradox that so offended and intrigued Rooney: that the people who are closest to the customer and who have the most influence on customer attitudes are given so few reasons, beyond their own basic decency, to create the positive, long-lasting relationships that companies say they crave. Rooney developed a soft spot for front line associates at Ameritech, one that he retains today. When he arrived at U.S. Cellular, he made the rehabilitation of these downtrodden groups one of his key priorities.

His constant presence and encouragement in the early days of the Dynamic Organization endeared him to the front lines, which became the first strongholds of support for change. The Dynamic Organization was a sales and service rep's dream come true. It put the customer's transactions with the rep at the very pinnacle of the company's strategic plan, gave them an unheard-of level of empowerment to make their own decisions in these customer encounters, promised them all the tools they needed to ensure positive outcomes, and afforded them the respect that they had never before enjoyed for doing their jobs.

The front lines embraced empowerment before they

understood it. In the headlong scramble to remake the company, no one noticed until too late that this value was too often being interpreted as a free-for-all. Sales and customer service reps did whatever they thought it took to make their customers happy. For some, this meant playing Santa Claus at the company's expense: giving away free phones or extra minutes, or waiving charges at the first hint of resistance. Instead of trying to resolve issues in a way that was fair to both company and customer—a process that involves attention to detail, problem-solving skill, and a measure of tact—associates were simply giving customers whatever they asked for, and then some. By the time their leaders realized that they were giving away millions of dollars worth of product and service each year, empowerment had become equated, in many minds, with the freedom to dispense company resources at will.

When senior leaders tried to put the horses back in the barn, establishing the boundaries and conditions and targets that should have been introduced from the beginning, it was too late, at least for a core of associates for whom the connection between customer focus and unfettered empowerment was by now sacrosanct. While most of the reps accepted the new limitations without qualm (many were, in fact, relieved to have some guidelines), this core group—which included some of the most experienced sales and service reps—resisted the changes, interpreting them as the company reneging on its initial promises.

Over time, these associates set themselves up as the customer's true champions. The company, they said, was reverting to its pre-Rooney instincts and putting profits ahead of customer satisfaction. They began to use the Dynamic Organization against the company, wrapping themselves in the "customer focus" mantle and using its protective powers to argue against any change that did not suit them. While appropriating the new culture's vocabulary, they subtly shifted the focus from the customer to themselves.

The episode proved that the best way to deal with a cultural cancer is to remove it.

These associates managed to wage a brilliant campaign of change resistance, using the Dynamic Organization itself as cover, and arguing passionately (and persuasively, to the many new recruits who came under their sway) that they, not their leaders, were the defenders of Jack's real intentions. They developed strongholds in key departments in several of the call centers—notably Roaming Support in Knoxville and National Resolutions in Tulsa—that took years to dismantle. The outright resistance of the Engineering group and the passive resentment of the staff areas were at least relatively straightforward and, once identified, easy to confront. Entitlement within the Sales and Customer Service organizations, however, was like a virus that had been injected into the Dynamic Organization itself, creating a persistent and hard to detect perversion of the nascent culture.

While this form of resistance would continue for at least another year or two, by 2004, the company was finally beginning to make some headway in dealing with it. Two developments made the most difference: a greater willingness to hold associates accountable for their behaviors, and a growing sophistication in understanding the respective roles of the customer and the associate in the company's business model.

For several years, associates had been complaining on the Culture Survey about the actions of the "bad apples" in their midst, the "takers" who used the system to their advantage without pulling their weight, and about the puzzling reluctance of their leaders to do something about them. These leaders, in turn, seemed unwilling to confront bad behavior, fearful that a firm hand might subject them to criticism on the next Culture Survey. The Human Resources department seemed just as reluctant to intervene, apparently oblivious to the fact that the bad apples were abusing the "respect" being accorded them.

A few individual leaders decided that they had had enough. The Wisconsin market was the company's largest, crucially important to U.S. Cellular's financial health, and the closest thing to a reliably well-oiled machine in the entire organization. The smart play, for a Wisconsin leader, was "don't mess things up." At the same time, Wisconsin associates had remained no more than lukewarm to Rooney and the Dynamic Organization. Protected by their traditionally strong sales performance, many Wisconsin associates thought that they could treat the new culture as an option, as long as their numbers were solid. Their lack of commitment to the D.O. (in some cases bordering on hostility) had created a poisonous atmosphere in one of the company's showcase markets, and a significant challenge to the culture's credibility.

Spurred by Rooney's demand that Wisconsin get off the fence, market leaders finally summoned the nerve to terminate their worst cases, including fifteen top sales performers. This action sent shock waves through U.S. Cellular; many believed that the company had just shot itself in the foot.

The actual result was a resounding demonstration of the importance of "how." Unencumbered by the nay-sayers whose selfish behavior frequently (as associates had for years been pointing out) disrupted an entire sales team, Wisconsin flourished, delivering better numbers than ever before and finally moving the needle on its Culture Survey results. The most important outcome of this episode, however, was to provide definitive proof to the rest of the organization that the best way to deal with a cultural cancer is to remove it.

Other markets and call centers began to follow that example, and the notion of associate accountability for the values and behaviors, as well as for results, gradually took root.

At the same time as the company was learning to deal more forthrightly with its "culture-killers," it was also developing a much more balanced appreciation of the relative roles of the customer and the associate in the Dynamic Organization's business model. Many associates had at first interpreted Customer Focus as an either-or choice: what was good for the customer was assumed to be bad for the company, and vice versa. Customer satisfaction or profits, one or the other—which will it be?

For several years, U.S. Cellular executives made slight headway in convincing associates that it was not only possible to have both, but necessary. They believed that the only way to get the business results that would allow the company to survive was through the customer. That part of the message resonated well with the organization. But it was just as important for associates to understand that the customer could not expect high quality products and services from a company that was not making money. That piece of the equation did not seem to penetrate nearly as easily.

Whenever U.S. Cellular sought to introduce a fee for a customer service, for example, associates resisted strongly, instinctively empathizing with their customers rather than accepting the company's justifications. When the company tried to include in its pricing plans the concept that premium service was worth paying for, the front lines again objected. The notion that the Dynamic Organization should benefit both the customer and the company seemed for years to be too counter-intuitive for most associates to embrace.

Gradually, however, years of patient teaching turned the tide. Leaders benefited from the expanding network of training programs that took the Business Model as their core text, and they were eventually able to spread these concepts to their teams. That associates could see for themselves these correlations at work helped to reinforce the lesson. Customers were obviously very happy with U.S. Cellular, and that had enabled the company to thrive beyond the wildest expectations of 2000; but it was also true that the company's success had enabled it to upgrade its network, improve its products and services, and modernize its systems and processes, all of which led to even greater customer satisfaction.

This slow realization that the customer and the company were mutually dependent, that what was good for one also helped the other, brought a new balance to associates' perceptions of the Dynamic Organization. This even-handedness robbed the resisters of much of their argument, which was based on the old either/or distinctions. With their peer audience less susceptible to their polarizing rhetoric, they began to lose their influence.

Not, however, in the strongholds. In a handful of those veteran-dominated locations, entitlement remained impervious to these encouraging developments. It would take something more—courageous leadership—to finally bring it down.

The Battle of Tulsa

Entitlement has been the illegitimate child of many well-intentioned attempts to take a humane approach to employee relations. The problem is epitomized by the workplace parable of the Thanksgiving turkey:

A beneficent CEO, appreciative of his employees and grateful for an excellent year, gave turkeys to his entire staff just before the Thanksgiving holiday. He was universally praised for his generosity. The next year was not as good for the business, and as Thanksgiving approached, turkeys were the last thing on the CEO's mind until he heard some grumbling about the company forgetting its people when times turned tough. He decided to keep the peace by again providing a holiday turkey. Each year the debate went on: did the company have a good enough year to buy a turkey? Each year, the trump card was employee expectations: what kind of signal would the CEO be sending if he ended the "turkey tradition"? Eventually, after a particularly difficult year, the executive team agreed on a compromise. Turkeys would still be provided, but they would be five pounds smaller, symbolizing the need for all to share in the necessary belt-tightening. Employees, of course, were enraged that the company would take advantage of the economic situation to cut "benefits." Morale plummeted and employee relations soured for years.

At U.S. Cellular, the Dynamic Organization's new emphasis on the importance of front-line associates as the gateway to customer satisfaction put an unaccustomed spotlight on the work environment and gave associates themselves a voice in shaping it. That led inevitably to excess, and then, gradually but inexorably, toward the belief, in some parts of the company, that the D.O. was really about associates more than it was about customers. Associates in these areas warned their leaders, sometimes explicitly, to "keep me satisfied, or I won't be in the right frame of mind to make my customers happy." U.S. Cellular had its very own turkey problem.

This sense of entitlement was apparent in every Customer Care Center by 2003, but nowhere had it become more entrenched than in Tulsa, a center that had been plagued more than most by a succession of weak leaders. Its most recent director—a newcomer to U.S. Cellular—had quickly adopted a strategy of trying to buy the affection of his troops with a non-stop succession of parties. It was fun while it lasted, which was less than six months. He left behind a snake pit, whose nerve center was the veteran core in National Resolutions.

National Resolutions dealt with the most complex customer issues and was staffed exclusively by experienced, savvy service reps who had seen it all, and who knew what a good thing they had in the D.O. For some of them, the affection was genuine. For many, however, the most important feature of the D.O. was the leverage it gave them in dealing with leaders. If they played their cards right, they could shape their work environment to suit themselves and then defend what they created by wrapping it in the banner of the D.O.

By the time Nancy Fratzke became Tulsa's director in 2004, these tenured associates had a strangle-hold on their center, which had by then developed a reputation for being virtually unmanageable. The best a new director could hope for, it was thought, was to find a way to accommodate the hard-liners before they ruined either her health or her career, if not both.

Fratzke came up through the call center ranks, starting as a service rep on the phones in the Knoxville center. She quickly became a respected coach and manager there, but she got the Tulsa job by default. The embarrassing tenure of the previous director had made another outside hire impossible, and the few experienced internal candidates took one look at the Tulsa mess and turned it down flat. When Fratzke accepted the job, expectations were muted on all sides.

She succeeded the same way all the other leaders described in this book succeeded: through personal example, painstaking one-on-one communication, and relentless focus on the Values and Behaviors, with all of these based on a deep foundation of genuine caring for her associates. These leaders were not working from a script, except perhaps by unconsciously following Rooney's own lead, but their collective experience helped develop the blueprint for what has eventually become U.S. Cellular's characteristically striving and granular approach to leadership.

The first thing that her new Tulsa team noticed about Fratzke was that she was right there on the call center floor with them, a visible presence unlike the office-bound, frequent-flying directors they were accustomed to. She learned their names. And not only that: she knew the names of their spouses and kids and pets as well. She seemed genuinely interested in them.

Even more striking, she did not disappear when the center was under pressure. Instead, she put on a head-set and started taking customer calls until the crisis was over. When the Culture Survey returned to Tulsa later that year, hundreds of associates wanted to talk about this amazing new director who actually rolled up her sleeves and got in the trenches with her troops. The entitlement crisis was far from over, but the first important lesson was in the air: that the D.O. is above all about serving the customer.

Fratzke underlined that message by putting an end to the "party on" strategy that her predecessors had followed: no more of the daily round of goodies and freebies that had marked the futile quest to buy associate "satisfaction." That move was unpopular, but it was not misunderstood. Fratzke proved to be an indefatigable communicator, meeting with her 400 or so associates and leaders on any topic that roiled the center, answering any question, repeating her customer-first message over and over in any context.

She won over her center one person at a time—by example, by persuasion, with tough love and discipline, and with the willingness, if necessary, to remove those who remained impervious to these efforts. She gradually built a team of managers and coaches who could reflect and extend her own approach. Many of these went on to lead other call centers and sales organizations within the company; several are still deployed regularly around the company as troubleshooters, or to help units that are struggling. She put so much of herself into her mission that associates began to worry about her, urging her to go home when she seemed to be exhausted.

Her reputation grew. Associates who had been leaders of the opposition a year earlier now joined the unofficial focus group competition to tell the most affecting Nancy-story: how, for example, she and Jon Lomax, one of her managers, had stayed until the center closed at 1 a.m. for weeks on end to make sure that a new night shift got off to a good start; how she and her leaders surprised associates by clearing their windshields when the center was hit by an ice storm.

> *"This has nothing to do with creating a workers' heaven. This is about delighting the customer."*
>
> —JACK ROONEY

Gradually the center began to turn. On the 2006 survey, when the call centers were in the depths of a deep funk caused by careless implementation of a new customer privacy policy that seemed to threaten associate job security, Tulsa provided a bright spot, generating superb results as well as some of the most heart-warming stories of the D.O. at its best. A year later, the triumphant 2007 survey proved that the center was still on a roll, not only numerically, but in the tone and quality of associate comments. One simply wrote that, as she looked out the window from her desk, wondering what she should write on the survey, she saw another call center in the distance and realized how unbelievably lucky she was to be working for U.S. Cellular.

Tulsa's focus group participants proved to be extraordinarily proud of their achievements and of the hard work and sacrifice that had produced them. If any new associate in the group seemed to be insufficiently aware of the center's history, their more-experienced co-workers were anxious to remind them.

During these interviews, something almost unimaginable a few years earlier happened regularly. A group of reps would express a difference of opinion on some culture-related issue, and after hearing the rival arguments, a veteran associate would introduce a calming, definitive comment by saying, "I'm from National Resolutions, and. . . ." That phrase had become a well-understood credential. It meant that the speaker had fought and lost the worst of U.S. Cellular's culture wars, but had emerged from battle with a hard-earned, bone-deep appreciation of the company, and the Dynamic Organization.

FROM 'ZERO' TO HERO

No sooner had the call centers begun to recover from their epic struggle with entitlement when they were hit between the eyes with "zero tolerance," an even more deadly threat to morale, customer focus, and associates' allegiance to the Dynamic Organization.

The zero tolerance story began harmlessly enough in early 2006, with the idea that U.S. Cellular should be doing more to guard the privacy of its customers. There had been a nationwide spike in highly publicized incidents of customers being harmed—sometimes physically—when other companies were careless about releasing personal information to unauthorized callers. Congress had developed an interest in the problem. Any organization that was truly customer focused needed to be on the right side of this issue.

U.S. Cellular had a long-standing policy in place to prevent such occurances, but it had become apparent that it was not being strictly followed. Requests had been made, warnings issued, to little avail. An executive stack or two blew, and an ill-considered e-mail blasted the calm of the Customer Care Centers, reaching the desks of most associates before their leaders had a chance to meet with them. Most of the message was fair and reasonable, but two words burrowed deep into the heart of the organization: "zero tolerance." Violators of the customer privacy policy would be terminated, period.

"Firestorm" would be far too mild a word to describe the reaction across the Customer Service department. For the next several months, the company tried to recover—defending, explaining, revising—to no avail. By the time of the 2006 Culture Survey, many associates had been terminated for violating the policy, and their peers' positions had hardened. As they saw it, the company had reneged on the value of respect, conducting a vendetta against its most loyal supporters; leaders were motivating not by values but by fear; the business model, with its reliance on satisfied associates to deliver a positive customer experience was a sham. Their response, in many cases, was to adopt a "me first" attitude, putting self-preservation well ahead of helping customers—any one of whom could now suddenly turn into a job threat.

In every center (except Tulsa, where Fratzke had characteristically led her managers onto the center floor in a marathon of team meetings to stem the tide of negative opinion), it was the same story: plunging morale and a much more negative perspective on jobs, leaders, the company as a whole. Survey results plummeted to reflect the dark new mood in the centers, a major reason for the overall decline in the culture that year.

What was even worse, this was the first crisis of Rooney's tenure that the company could not seem to fix with its usual formula of leadership grit and determination. Senior leaders made several grudging adjustments to the policy's draconian enforcement, but these just added confusion to the mix. Executives toured the centers to meet with associates and offer tentative apologies—but only for the awkward implementation and the insensitive communication. Several centers conducted midyear culture reviews in January of 2007 to see if these half-measures had stopped the bleeding. They had not.

On the 2007 survey, nearly eighteen months after the original gaffe, zero tolerance was still the number one topic of conversation in the centers. While newly-appointed associates were generally unaffected by the controversy, and some veteran reps had succeeded in moving past their concerns, many more seemed to feel that an important line had been permanently crossed. U.S. Cellular was still a good company to work for, but the Camelot era of the Dynamic Organization was over. The magic was gone. This was just a job after all.

What a disaster! The company devotes years to building a customer focused culture, succeeds beyond any expectation, and just at the point where victory is within its grasp, one of the most critical components of the front line organization collapses in a pile of self-protective recrimination. The sad episode seemed like it could be a potentially fatal blow to the D.O.

When Lynn Costlow arrived on the scene, no one knew she was the cavalry. Hardly anyone knew her at all, in fact. She had been an outside consultant to the company for several years. Her work had impressed the company to the point where she was put in charge of the Sales Operations group, where she made a reputation as a quick study of the culture that had so often tripped up outsiders. But when she took over as Vice President of the call centers in late 2007, there was little reason to think that she was the right person to confront one of the company's most serious threats.

She was. She shared some of the same traits that have characterized the D.O.'s best leaders: the willingness to confront a problem head on and face-to-face; a commitment to wide-open communications, wherever it leads; and indomitable courage. She barnstormed every call center, engaged with every leader, met every associate. She told them she knew nothing about their world, but promised that she would learn it fast. Her honesty allowed her to connect with people on an emotional level; within a couple of months she had at least recaptured the department's attention.

Her priority was to change the subject, to distract her organization from the topic that had obsessed it for so long and refocus its attention on the customer once more. Rooney had originally used the customer as the lever to shift the company's gaze from inside to outside; Costlow would do the same thing to get the department's mind off the policies and regulations that had hijacked center stage.

She convened a meeting of every leader in the department, and turned them loose to create a new vision and mission for Customer Service, a statement that would reenergize their commitment to the ideal customer experience. Then, armed with her leaders' work, she hit the road again, using a town hall meeting format to bring her messages to the reps.

She had two main goals: she needed to put the customer

back in the center of the call center universe; and she wanted to convince her audience that, once again, they were special—the essential link between company and customer, the cornerstone of Rooney's strategy, the difference-makers between U.S. Cellular and everybody else. She told the call centers that they "had to get their mojo back" for the company to succeed.

Every U.S. Cellular executive conducts Straight Talks—free-flowing give-and-take are the centerpiece of the company's communication strategy. Costlow's town hall sessions took that openness to a new level of absolute frankness. "What sucks today?" she would ask a group of reluctant participants, and the questions and opinions would pour out. No topic was off-limits; nothing was routed into the "parking lot;" no punches were pulled in her responses. She readily admitted what she didn't know but always circled back when she had done her homework.

Associates, as one coach observed, "fell in love with her." They saw how much she cared about them and their work, the driving passion she brought to a frenetic schedule, not unlike Jack Rooney himself. This chemistry enabled the call centers finally to turn the page, reminding the service reps in the process of what had made them love their work and their company so much in the first place.

Costlow's achievement is still in its early stages. However, the positive signs are unmistakable. There is a noticeable change in the department's mood. Associates and leaders are smiling again, teams are having fun, and there is once again a buzz of energy in the centers.

The 2008 Culture Survey provided tangible evidence of the turnaround. Customer Service's results returned dramatically to form, announcing the end of its two-year funk. The entire department was recognized for Dynamic Leadership at that year's Leadership Forum, as Network Operations/Engineering had been in 2007. The cheers of their peers represented more than well-earned recognition for Costlow and her leaders; they also signaled the whole company's relief that one of U.S. Cellular's most critical components was back on the team.

THE PERENNIAL
PULL OF THE ORDINARY

The 2006 Leadership Conference was a sobering lesson that the Dynamic Organization cannot afford to rest on its laurels. Until then, each year's Culture Survey results had been better than the last, and in 2004 and 2005 they were so significantly better that it seemed the company was gathering inexorable forward momentum. Some of the setbacks recorded in 2006 were the result of missteps already recounted, such as the "zero tolerance" policy, and the mishandled E-911 recall. Others had less to do with specific incidents than with developing patterns—a burgeoning bureaucracy and some thoughtless backsliding into the ordinary on the part of a company that had set its sites on being nothing less than extraordinary. These patterns have their roots in some of the most common features of human and organizational nature. For that reason, the lessons they teach seem never seem to be permanently learned. Even now, some of these same forces keep reemerging, forming a regular threat to the culture, as persistent as spring floods.

GROWTH AND THE INNER BUREAUCRAT

The essence of the Dynamic Organization is the individual, one-on-one transaction between the customer and a front-line associate empowered to do what it takes to create an "ideal" experience. The company's role is to provide everything necessary—effective leaders, empathetic support staff, the requisite tools, training, and information—to make such transactions consistent and predictable. Whatever impedes or distracts from them is the enemy, and needs to be rooted out with vigilance.

That is the goal, and a company capable of achieving it necessarily looks very different than most organizations. For one thing, most of the forces at work in this model are centrifugal. Regional leadership pulls decision-making away from top management and closer to the customer, and as many of those decisions as possible are delegated to the front line leaders and associates who know their customers best. "Headquarters" turns into a Regional Support Organization. Leaders get out of their offices, roll up their sleeves, and spend their time in the trenches, leading from the front.

This is a fundamentally anti-bureaucratic vision, one that U.S. Cellular has, for the most part, successfully implemented. The company did not notice for some time that there were some powerful influences within the organization that were driving it, unconsciously for the most part, in the opposite direction. Those forces have periodically become so strong that they have threatened—and still do—to break down the unique character of the D.O. model and turn U.S. Cellular back into something more conventional, more comfortable, a little easier.

There is probably nothing sinister in all this. It may be no more than a form of natural regression to the mean. Many people are uncomfortable with being outliers and going against the grain of convention. They react to their discomfort through a tendency to return to the typical, the tried-and-true. Examples are easy to find, even on Rooney's senior team. At that level, of course, their impact, intentional or not, can be huge.

Such individuals may share, at least on an intellectual level, the pride in the D.O.'s uniqueness and in U.S. Cellular's courageous march to its own drumbeat, but their hearts push them inexorably back to the comforts of the familiar. They become, without fully realizing it, double agents, threatening the culture from within by turning it slowly, imperceptibly, and unintentionally into the D.O.'s worst fear: an ordinary company.

This problem first emerged early in Rooney's tenure, when the company was frantically engaged in two massive, parallel efforts: to change the culture, and to bring its internal systems and processes into the 21st century. The latter task was just as wrenching as the former, and it preoccupied the staff groups in the RSO for years—so much so that some of them may have failed to notice that they were no longer in sole charge of the company.

During this period of rebuilding its infrastructure, the

phrase "operational excellence" took on new resonance. This had always been part of U.S. Cellular's vocabulary, but now, with the new emphasis on process, and with the further impetus provided by Sarbanes-Oxley, the words took on more weight, providing a buttoned-down counterweight to the more freewheeling tendencies of an empowered front line.

Many leaders pointed out that if Jack Rooney had ever accepted "it is what it is," the D.O. would never have seen the light of day. "It" is not what it is. "It" can be something much better than that.

This was a healthy development, and probably essential to the company's survival. It was obvious to even the most freedom-loving associate that the company could not continue to compete in a consolidating industry as the loose federation of undisciplined fiefdoms that it had been in the past. Rooney wanted every representative of the company to "look like U.S. Cellular." A store in Bangor, Maine should seem as familiar to a wide-ranging customer as one in Wichita Falls, Texas or the Chicago Loop.

It was just as evident that the "ideal customer experience" required more than the day-to-day creativity of several thousand front line associates. It also needed consistency and predictability, and that meant operational excellence.

So far so good. The entire company was grateful for the contributions of staff departments like Marketing, Sales Operations, the new shared-services group (Business Support Services), and the even newer Customer Service Organization, which centralized many of the planning activities previously performed by the individual call centers. Through their efforts, the company was gradually achieving Rooney's goal of creating a consistent, identifiable U.S. Cellular look and feel.

The problem that no one saw coming had two distinct aspects, neither of them good for the D.O. The first of these was the unintended impact all the new programs were having on the front line organizations. There were so many of them, coming from so many different directions, that front line leaders suddenly found themselves overwhelmed with the administrative requirements of a growing company: three or four conference calls a day, meetings, training programs, an avalanche of email, coaching sessions, development plans, an endless stream of reports.

Leaders with a strong inner bureaucrat found it easy to justify spending entire days and weeks behind shut office doors, or away from their teams altogether, attending the expanding number of conferences and planning meetings and training courses. Those who were tempted to ignore these demands on their time found that they were as accountable for their paperwork and conference call participation as they were for their coaching responsibilities, which remained as demanding as ever. Associates sympathized with leaders who were "stretched transparent" or "held hostage," and pleaded for their release.

By 2006, the situation had reached crisis proportions. Many associates, seeing their leaders pulled in so many conflicting directions, decided they wanted no part of leadership. Front line leaders themselves were frantic, working too many hours to try to fit everything in, feeling guilty about letting down their teams, or worrying that they were risking their

futures by giving short shrift to their administrative responsibilities—and sometimes all three at once. That year, these
"missing in action" leaders were one of the main topics of discussion in the focus groups.

The second aspect of the problem followed inevitably
from the first. As front line leaders, distracted and overwhelmed, unconsciously surrendered the power and influence that Rooney had intended for them, the resulting
vacuum was quickly filled by the very staff people who had
devised the programs and created the standards and built
this emerging bureaucracy. This transfer of power was largely
unplanned, a byproduct of the unannounced change in organizational priorities. There was certainly no malice involved.
The staff groups, for the most part, were as appreciative of
the D.O., Rooney's business model, and what these had done
for U.S. Cellular as anyone.

Still, the effect was unmistakeable: headquarters was back
in charge, and with a bit of an attitude. The 2006 survey was
inundated by complaints from front line leaders about the
lack of input they were allowed in the programs that were
changing their lives, the poor communication that left them
without the "whys" they needed to explain them to their
people, the whiff of arrogance they detected in some quarters. In more than a few cases, the flood of new requirements
seemed to have as much to do with ticking off "to do" items
on the internal agendas of staff groups as they did with serving the front lines or helping the customer.

All these frustrations were summed up in a massive rejec-
tion of a phrase that had been widely used in the RSO that year
to deflect the questions that were supposed to be the D.O.'s

life's blood: "It is what it is." That non-response was intended to shut down dialog and put the questioner in his/her place. The clear message was, "Don't waste your time or mine; just do what you're told," and it provoked an insurrection on the survey. Many leaders pointed out that if Jack Rooney had ever accepted "it is what it is," the D.O. would never have seen the light of day. Others argued that the whole spirit of the D.O. was the very opposite of that put-down. "It" is *not* what it is. "It" can be something much better than that.

Outbreaks of out-of-control bureaucracy do not just happen at random, like natural disasters. They have human causes: namely leadership or its absence.

That reaction stopped the power shift in its tracks, at least temporarily. The immediate outcome was a good-faith attempt, right across the company, to get the incipient bureaucracy under control and free front line leaders to lead again. Whole regions went on the warpath against "clutter," and staff departments made a greater effort to gather front line input and to coordinate their new programs and systems with each other. The front line's capacity to absorb change became a key criterion in planning. Gradually, leaders were able to get back to their teams. The offending phrase disappeared from the U.S. Cellular lexicon.

That happy outcome was not, unfortunately, the end of the story. The cheers of the 2007 Leadership Forum had barely died down before the old pattern started to re-emerge. By the first months of 2008, the out-of-control work loads of front line leaders were again threatening to overwhelm the delicate balance of the D.O. ecosystem, and the senior leader team was forced to convene a special session just to deal with the crisis.

On the surface, it looked as if some staff groups, with a major rebranding of the company looming just months away, simply got carried away with a natural desire to clean up every last bit of organizational litter before the launch. There is no doubt some truth in that analysis. But closer inspection revealed that a major source of the deluge was the inability of some RSO leaders and their teams to control the bureaucratic impulse. Some of the new programs that were doing much of the damage at the front lines turned out to have nothing to do with the rebranding. Their sponsors were either supremely insensitive to the company's priorities, or saw the general pre-occupation as an opportunity to advance a departmental (or even a personal) agenda item or two.

There is a school of thought that none of this should be particularly disturbing, that these episdoes are simply part of an endless cycle, an ongoing pendulum swing that a growing company in a competitive marketplace is bound to endure. Periods of intense internal focus are necessary to give the organization a chance to catch up on its homework, according to this view, before it turns its full attention outward again to its customers and front line associates.

The Dynamic Organization's more passionate support-ers disagree. The company's business model tells them that outbreaks of out-of-control bureaucracy do not just happen at random, like natural disasters. They have human causes: namely leadership or its absence. They represent a surrender to the gravitational forces that are always working to pull the culture down to earth, a failure to "defend the D.O." and its uniqueness, an acquiescence to the ordinary, the thin edge of a potentially fatal wedge. From this perspective, the proper response to bureaucracy is not to accept it or coexist with it, or wait for it to go away, but to eradicate it.

Rooney, as usual, may have the last word. He has always believed that the D.O. is designed for heavy lifting of all kinds. Plenty of less demanding cultures are capable of generating garden-variety results under routine conditions. U.S. Cellular has not spent the better part of a decade mobilizing the hearts and minds of its entire workforce just to do the ordinary. It now has at its disposal a truly unique instrument that should be capable of developing a creative solution to the knottiest business problems, such as having the benefits of bureaucracy without its intolerable costs.

The company's choice in this matter, therefore, is not either/or: either bureaucracy or customer-focus, either piston-like consistency or the capacity for inspiration. A Dynamic Organization should at this point be capable of both, of finding a way to have it all: the comforts of predictability and efficiency as well as the unique and irreplaceable advantages of associate engagement and customer intimacy.

THE POWER OF THE RUBBER BAND

Of the hard lessons encountered on U.S. Cellular's path, the most difficult of all deals with the basic question of the human capacity for change. Any change initiative is premised on the assumption that, with enough information and appropriate motivation, most people are capable of making fundamental alterations in their behavioral patterns and, ultimately, in their belief structures. The Dynamic Organization and all its support systems are built on that assumption, and Rooney's many successes indicate that it is essentially correct.

Essentially. But not, apparently, universally, and certainly not easily or quickly. After years of effort at U.S. Cellular, after all the company's incredible achievements, after all the heart-warming and inspirational examples of individual and organizational transformation that have marked this prog-ress, and long after the evidence that the D.O. represents a better way has been clear and irrefutable—after all that, there is still a stubborn intransigence in some people, a persistent, sub-conscious pull of old, discredited habits that is as strong as a force of nature. The tide goes out—and surely the broad expanse of beach left behind is an improvement over the unruly waves it seems to replace—and then a few hours later the darn wet stuff returns, as oblivious to our sand castles and beach blankets as ever.

Myra Kruger likens culture change to a rubber band. The organization pulls on the band, and it stretches, taking new shapes and forms. But as soon as the organization relaxes and lets up the pressure, the band returns to its original form, leav-ing no evidence of its previous contortions. Many people, and therefore many groups, seem to have the same tendency. They give the appearance of real change, as long as there is sufficient external pressure, but when they are left to their own devices, they revert to their old habits. The new shape was an illusion.

This is why complacency is such a devastating enemy of change. A little success encourages people to ease the pressure, and before they are aware of it, they have lost what they had gained. The only answer is to have the courage to keep stretching that band. When it snaps, it may hurt a bit, and even cause some disorder, but only then can the individual, and the team, be free from the pull of the past.

Examples of the rubber band effect abound at U.S. Cellular. One of the most frustrating was the Wisconsin market, one of the company's largest and most profitable, but for many years a stubborn holdout from Rooney and the D.O. The problem was Wisconsin's past. Most of the Wisconsin staff had spent their careers with Bell South, a company that regarded itself as elite, even among the rapidly dwindling Baby Bells. U.S. Cellular had bought the market just prior to Rooney's arrival—a transition that was poorly received. Bell South had been a wealthy, sophisticated parent. U.S. Cellular was an upstart country cousin: "Jethro Cellular," as it became known to its new acquisition. It was like being adopted by the Beverly Hillbillies. Then came Rooney, whose Ameritech background impressed them only slightly more than U.S. Cellular. Whatever this Dynamic Organization of his was about, it couldn't possibly be as good as what they had known at Bell South. Those years now took on all the sentimental aura of a lost Golden Age, with which their current employer could not hope to compete.

Wisconsin's leaders mastered the art of passive resistance. They held themselves aloof to the waves of change that were rocking the company, surreptitiously mocking the efforts of Rooney and his team. They learned how to appear invisible on the annual culture survey, regularly producing results that were neither good enough nor bad enough to attract an unwelcome spotlight. Their clear preference was to be left alone with their memories.

The Wisconsin market's arrogance infuriated Rooney, who is not the "leaving alone" type. The state was the scene of a number of the CEO's "magenta moments," memorable explosions that did little to change minds, but at least got the market's attention. Heads rolled, eventually. A "year of fear" reminded leaders that resisting change was not an option, although it did little to improve the culture. A few bright spots emerged here and there, but by 2005, Wisconsin still represented the last major frontier for the Dynamic Organization.

That year, the market's Director of Sales—a long-time symbol of the Bell South era—sensed that the jig was up, and announced his own conversion to the D.O. His support signaled that it was now permissible for Wisconsin to join the company, and on that year's survey, it recorded its best-ever results. All of U.S. Cellular exulted in the capitulation. The Director of Sales immediately went on tour to explain to appreciative audiences across the company the secrets of successful culture change.

Some of that change was genuine. Over the previous five years, many Wisconsinites had come to appreciate what Rooney and U.S. Cellular were doing, and they wanted to be part of it. Those who had joined the company since 2000 had no memory of the old days and were becoming, quite frankly, a little tired of the Bell South stories. There is no doubt that, having made the leap, even many of the former resisters felt good, finally, to be part of a larger entity and to be able to contribute to it. From then on, Wisconsin gradually became one of the company's most reliable sources of leadership.

But the change didn't take. Believing that they had finally

"cracked the code" of the D.O., many Wisconsin leaders stopped pulling on the rubber band. Just when the market thought it had completed its victory lap, the rubber band reverted to its true shape, and after the disappointing 2006 survey results, Wisconsin was left to ponder what had happened to the breakthrough that it had assumed was permanent. This experience provided a healthy shock and, at least temporarily, moved the market past its crippling complacency. The Director of Sales, disappointed that still more effort was going to be required, left the company. He was replaced by Chris Rathsack, a Wisconsin native son and one of the D.O.'s true believers, who is painstakingly helping his team understand the dynamics of the rubber band.

Culture change is like a rubber band. The organization pulls on the band, and it stretches, taking new shapes and forms. But as soon as the organization relaxes and lets up the pressure, the band returns to its original form.

The same thing happened in neighboring Iowa. After Don Cochran led that market out of its perennial underachiever status to become one of the D.O.'s showcases, his successor embarked on a popularity contest that played to her team's old, undisciplined habits. Boinnng! The rubber band snapped back with a vengeance, leaving the market with a leadership void and the task of rebuilding the D.O. from the ground up.

Two of the company's earliest successes—Nick Wright's old East North Carolina unit and the Oregon/California market of Kathy Hust and Denise Hutton—fell on similar hard times under leaders who lacked the courage and the drive to keep the pressure on the rubber band. In both cases the markets felt betrayed, as strong teams who had taken great pride in their accomplishments saw their units lose their sense of direction and, almost imperceptibly, their leadership position within the company.

Progress rarely occurs in a straight line. It happens when the forward zigs eventually and decisively outnumber the backward zags.

None of these markets fell apart. All of them are today in recovery, regaining their balance, reestablishing momentum. They all have the benefit, at least, of knowing what hit them, and the opportunity not to make the same mistake again. But the ubiquity of the problem is a reason for caution. The same phenomenon has occurred so often that it appears to be built in to the change process itself. Based on these experiences, it would seem reasonable to conclude that progress rarely occurs in a straight line. It happens when the forward zigs eventually and decisively outnumber the backward zags.

Mistakes happen, especially under pressure. The company made a doozy in 2006 with the "zero tolerance" fiasco in the call centers. And yet, with that example still reverberating and the culture in the centers still far from full recovery, it fell into the same trap eighteen months later when it introduced a similar customer privacy protection policy to the sales organization. The leaders who made the decision knew the history, and they had plenty of time to avoid a repeat, yet they created an almost identical distraction the second time around. How could that happen?

If these mishaps had occurred in almost any other company, no one would be very much surprised: just another instance of some corporate executive going off the rails. Happens every day. But at U.S. Cellular, the Dynamic Organization provides fool-proof guidelines to take the personal pressure off any would-be decision-maker: What will be the impact on the customer? Is this consistent with the Values and Behaviors? So perhaps the question here is not "how could a mistake like zero tolerance happen?" but rather "why is it so hard to keep those D.O. guidelines in mind—and in force?"

When you examine the particulars, the answer appears to take us back to the rubber band. Many of Rooney's leaders have demonstrated the capacity for real change. They pulled the band, and pulled it well past the points of discomfort, of stress, of fear of the unknown. They have kept pulling, no matter what, until it broke, and they became truly different people than they had been. That kind of change—the first half of Rooney's famous "change people or change people" dictum—is possible.

But it is also elusive. Some of the most endangering situations for the culture have been created—and still are—by leaders who have been with Rooney the longest, or by leaders who were among the Dynamic Organization's most storied early converts. They know what the culture requires, they understand its standards, they know by heart the questions they should be asking. But then, when the chips are down, they revert to some older, pre-D.O. version of themselves. The rubber band returns to a shape that is out of place in this culture.

Every book needs at least one sports analogy. Here is ours:

Slugger and future Baseball Hall of Famer Manny Ramirez is famously eccentric, creating one distraction after another for his teams. But he hits so well that all is inevitably forgiven.

No leader is bigger than the D.O., or there is no D.O.

The phrase "That's just Manny being Manny" is the all-purpose excuse, even if his behavior would result in a lesser talent being banished to the minors. We have heard variations on the "Manny being Manny" theme at U.S. Cellular, used by apologists to excuse a flagrantly self-centered or otherwise out-of-bounds action by a powerful leader. It doesn't work there. Manny can't be Manny, unless that means being customer focused, ethical, respectful, and so on. No leader is bigger than the D.O., or there is no D.O.

Rooney knows this. It is why, at the peak of the culture's strength during the triumphant 2007 Leadership Forum, he implored his leaders to defend the D.O., to have the awareness to recognize and the courage to confront any behavior that harms the culture, no matter who the perpetrator. Sometimes, he was saying, we need to save what we love best from ourselves. When key leaders are failing to apply their fair share of pressure to the rubber band, others in the organization must call them out.

Maybe a more reliable approach to change is to put greater faith in the second half of Rooney's equation: ". . . or change people." If changing people—really fundamentally altering their core qualities to make them fit the D.O.—is so hard, perhaps the more lasting solution is to look for replacements who already have the right stuff, those who already fit the culture without fundamental alterations. Hiring outsiders brought mixed results during the first years of the D.O., but the company has long since learned how to find and select people who are capable of making a seamless transition. Many of the leaders who have made the most valuable recent contributions to the D.O. fit that description, people like Jeff Childs and Lynn Costlow.

Whatever approach U.S. Cellular takes in the future, it has learned that the greatest barrier to change is the sheer difficulty of change itself. Real culture change requires more than compliance or conformity or cosmetics, although they certainly represent a start. It is not enough to be "on board" or to appear "dynamic." Real change requires something more, another level beyond mere appearance. The company's most amazing achievement is that it has enabled thousands of people to change in that way. The risks they have taken—all those broken rubber bands!—make it imperative that the company accept no less from any of its leaders.

PART 4

Taking it
to the Streets

INSIDE-OUT:
WHAT YOU SEE IS
WHO WE ARE

All of us have become cynics. We had no choice: cynicism is the only way we can survive the barrage, the avalanche, the tidal wave of exaggerations, fabrications, and outright lies we are told every day, in our roles as consumers, employees, and citizens. We are lied to so routinely that it is now almost impossible to shock us. Bring it on, tell us your most outrageous whoppers, spin your most extravagant sales pitches! It doesn't matter—we don't believe any of it.

Politics is partly to blame. Even the most well-intentioned politicians feel impelled, at some point, to promise something that clearly will never be delivered, and maybe not even attempted. We don't mind the subterfuge. We're cynics. We may hope our political leaders will tell us the truth, and occasionally one seems to try; but we know better than to expect it as a steady diet.

And advertising—don't get us started! The drug commercials that envelop the evening news programs promise pharmacological miracles, plus a nifty life-style, at least until they get to the disclaimers, which often run longer than the promises. And even then, we've learned the hard way that the wonder-product is quite capable of packing an ugly surprise. Today's miracle is, far too often, tomorrow's recall.

The worst thing that could happen would be to put a public stake in the ground and then fail to measure up.

Still, in spite of the number of times we've been burnt, some of the lies stick, especially if they are well-packaged and confidently told.

Enron was, right up to the final months before it was revealed as a house of particularly shoddy cards, one of the most admired companies in the country (#18 on the *Fortune* list in 2002. In the same issue, it was named, with astonishing prescience, "the most innovative company in America"). Even our practiced cynicism was no match for an extraordinarily effective hype machine.

If we let our guard down for even a minute, we're sure to get in trouble. For all our wariness, we've participated in two huge economic bubbles (Internet and real estate) within ten years, inflicting enormous damage on the economy, not to mention household budgets. We fell in love with the shiny surface, mistook the glossy exterior for reality, and forgot Survival Rule Number One: Don't believe anybody who wants to sell you something.

We have reached, in fact, a kind of marketplace stalemate. On one side are the sellers and their stories, told through devilishly clever public relations and advertising strategies. The stories, sad experience has taught us, are usually misleading or false. The external appeal is almost never a fair reflection of the internal reality. On the other side are the customers, armed with our hard-won cynicism, but severely handicapped by our desire to believe, our deep-down wish that every now and then one of those tall tales might turn out to be true.

Sometimes the sellers win. Their story is just too good, or our need to believe gets the better of us. Sometimes we customers successfully resist, sending the sellers back to the drawing board. Somehow most of us survive, except for the unfortunate consumers who fall too hard and lose their homes or their health or their nest eggs, or the sellers who push their stories too far over the line of criminal conduct.

Thank God there are exceptions, oases where we can shed our cynicism and allow ourselves to believe once again. Most of these are members of the well-known pantheon of modern commerce: the Nordstroms and Starbucks and Southwest Airlines of the world, case-studied obsessively for their peculiar habits of honest dealing. In these companies, the external image and the internal reality almost always coincide. The customer experience is as good as they tell us it will be. We can safely, for the moment, lower our defenses and believe again.

Where do these wonderful exceptions come from? In most cases, they originate in the DNA of their founders. Their values and habits derive from an original visionary, who controlled the company long enough to stamp the culture in his/ her image. Herb Kelleher of SWA; Isadore Sharp of the Four Seasons Hotels; Howard Shultz of Starbucks: their ideas, their companies, their cultures, through and through. Inside, outside, no difference. Those companies are what they say they are. Furthermore, they have always been that way. Their direction was set in infancy, and they never deviated from it as they grew. If they did happen to wander briefly from the trail, they soon found their way again.

There are very few cases of companies achieving that result—seamless consistency between the talk and the walk—without the benefit of a visionary parent and a focused upbringing. Many mature companies have tried to make the changes necessary to bring external image and internal reality into alignment, but hardly any have succeeded. The sad history of corporate culture change is littered with corpses: organizations that gave it a go, spent a lot of money, and finally gave up. Most of them were forced to recognize that it is far more cost-effective to do what everybody else does: leave the intractable culture, the bedrock internal reality of the company, alone; focus on external image instead.

Through Mythos, the company's brand would become its culture, and its culture would finally become the brand.

This book is the story of one of the rare exceptions. U.S. Cellular's public image in 2000 was spotty, to put it charitably. It was well known in the small towns and rural areas where it was generally the dominant (if not the only) provider, but beyond those boundaries it barely registered on the public consciousness. As the eighth largest wireless company in a rapidly shrinking field, it was widely assumed to be destined for oblivion. Few would have missed it. Even where it had name recognition, the company was not associated with any particular quality, except, perhaps, for an aversion to leading its industry at anything. Its own employees derided its commitment to being a follower, and not even a fast one. U.S. Cellular was noted for nothing in particular—not low prices, not great service, not high reliability. The epitome of its promotional efforts was the "penny phone," always a sure-fire crowd-pleaser.

Its nebulous public identity, back then, was a fairly accurate reflection of the kind of company it actually was: nondescript, undistinguished, and unlikely to leave much trace in the rather likely event of its demise. This congruence of internal and external reality was certainly more appealing than the situation at many of its big-spending competitors, where an expensively-purchased image often masked a truly repellant culture, but it was not a situation likely to help the company survive. Something obviously needed to change. The conventional play would have been to put as many resources as possible into creating a stronger, more attractive public image premised on a new, improved, customer-loving U.S. Cellular. If that ploy worked, it might generate enough growth to fund a few internal improvements, and it would likely buy Rooney and his lieutenants enough time to be able to claim credit for a "turnaround" and make a stock option killing. This, of course, is the tried-and-true model that routinely churns out rich CEOs and cynical consumers.

Rooney, as we have seen, had a different approach in mind—its polar opposite, in fact. His entire focus for the next few years would be on changing the culture, the most internal reality there is, the very marrow of the company. In that time, the transformation of U.S. Cellular was total. What it valued, what it believed, what it thought, how it acted—everything

about it was not only different, but unequivocally better by
every measure than it had been: better for customers, for associates, for shareholders, for communities. By 2008, there is no
doubt in the minds of any who know the company that it has
succeeded wonderfully in building something new, different,
and important.

In a mind-boggling reversal of conventional corporate
wisdom, through these years of real change, real improvement,
real difference, the company paid relatively little attention to
its brand image. For associates, this stubborn modesty began
as a mild irritant that became more upsetting with every passing year. As their awareness of the company's uniqueness and
their pride in their accomplishment grew, they became impatient to tell the story to a wider audience. Being the industry's
"best kept secret" became less a point of pride than a source of
growing consternation that U.S. Cellular was not doing more
to tout its differences from other companies.

A rising tide of survey comments expressed frustration with
the company's advertising approach, which continued to focus
almost exclusively on price, plans, and sales promotions, exactly
like every other wireless carrier. Its TV commercials seemed to
strive for a quirky and self-deprecating effect. The better the
company became, the less effective its advertising and marketing strategies seemed to be in pointing out its real virtues.
According to its associates (and many of its customers), there
was just as wide a gap between image and reality at U.S. Cellular as at any of its peers, except that in this company, the gap
was reversed: the reality was far superior to the public image.

The last straw for many associates came when much of
the wireless industry belatedly got on the customer band-

wagon. Companies with a well-earned reputation for indifference suddenly seemed to comprehend the wisdom of
befriending the consumer. Major carriers developed new
customer-centric campaigns, posing as their customers' new
best friends. U.S. Cellular associates may have been flattered
by the imitation at first, but that reaction soon turned to
outrage. These companies were claiming to be something
they were not, while their own com-
pany seemed oblivious that its hard-
earned thunder was being stolen.

This angst reached its peak
over rival claims to have the "best
network." U.S. Cellular had made
network excellence a key criterion
of the customer focus value, and was
immensely proud of the recognition
that had signaled its success. The
company won award after award
from local news media and industry

> *"We should be proud.*
> *We shold be able to say,*
> *'Boy, what a wonder-*
> *ful company!' We have*
> *to feel that ourselves to*
> *convince anyone else."*
>
> —JACK ROONEY

sources. *Consumer Reports* magazine recognized it for
generating far fewer complaints, per capita, than any other
carrier. Independent drive-testing confirmed the extraordinary
reliability of its coverage. In the face of this overwhelming
evidence of their own network's superiority, associates were
forced to witness Verizon, Cingular/AT&T, Sprint/Nextel,
and even Alltel claiming to have the best national network
or the most powerful network or the fewest dropped calls.
Each of these claims is possible only through the careful use
of weasel-words. "National" disqualifies a regional carrier
like U.S. Cellular from the comparison, for example, and

"powerful" says nothing about quality, but there they are, on television and billboards and full-page newpaper ads day after day. U.S. Cellular, meanwhile, made only an occasional perfunctory reference to its own clear superiority, seemingly content to let customers discover the truth for themselves.

There was a reason why U.S. Cellular seemed so maddeningly passive about telling its story. Rooney didn't think it was ready. He was more aware than anyone of the progress the organization had made, the growing strength of the culture, and the competitive advantage it was creating for the company. But the Dynamic Organization was not fully installed by 2004, the year of the first breakthrough on the Culture Survey, or by 2005, when the survey results reached even greater heights. For all the good news, there were still too many exceptions, too many rough edges, too many key items still on his "to do" list. U.S. Cellular was providing a far better customer experience than any of its competitors, but it was not yet "ideal." Until it was, Rooney was reluctant to go public with his company's achievement. The worst thing that could happen, he thought, would be to put a public stake in the ground and then fail to measure up. Making claims that his associates could not consistently back up—in every store, from every associate, with no exceptions or bad days or excuses—would be a bigger mistake, in his mind, than making no claims at all. If any of his people fell short, customers would be disappointed. They might think that there was really no difference between U.S. Cellular and the rest of the field after all, that its claims were just another corporate come-on. If that happened, all the gains of the previous few years might be short-lived. It could take years more to recover. And besides, it just would not be the right thing to do.

The setbacks that undermined the 2006 survey results proved Rooney's prescience. The company was not ready—not quite. But its reaction—the willingness of leaders across the organization to roll up their sleeves and renew their efforts on behalf of the culture—was the right one, and when the 2007 findings showed how successful they had been, Rooney finally agreed that the time was ripe for a coming-out party.

That occasion would be as painstakingly planned as every other phase of U.S. Cellular's evolution. The vehicle for turning the company inside-out—for revealing to the outside world exactly what kind of a company this was—was Project Mythos, the brainstorm of John Coyle, a brilliant young marketer who understood the power of the story his front line colleagues had been creating for years. "Mythos" is the Greek word for story or legend, and Project Mythos would be U.S. Cellular's opportunity to tell its collective story, and the thousands of individual stories that had shaped its culture. Through Mythos, the company's brand would become its culture, and its culture would finally become the brand. The internal reality would become the external identity. A 2007 survey participant described this process as "taking what's inside U.S. Cellular to the outside," and then "showing it to the world." What the world saw of U.S. Cellular would not be an ad agency fantasy or an executive's wishful thinking. It would be, finally, what this company really is.

OUTSIDE-IN: LEARNING TO BREATHE

Before U.S. Cellular could turn itself inside-out for all the world to see, it had to get its inmost recesses ready for the most exacting kind of 24/7, microscopes-and-spotlights inspection. Preparation required a total transformation: the arduous process we have described in this book. In previous chapters, we have focused on several of the critical elements of this process: customer focus, leadership, doing the right thing. Just as important for an appreciation of the magnitude of this achievement is a sense of the arc of the process itself, a boomerang-like trajectory that began outside U.S. Cellular, penetrated right to its heart, then re-emerged years later as an extraordinary force for positive change that extends far beyond the company itself.

"Believe that your work is noble and good things will follow."

—JACK ROONEY

In the beginning, the Dynamic Organization was a foreign idea, imported into U.S. Cellular by an uninvited change agent whose personal style, thought processes, and expectations all seemed excessive to much of the company, and most of its leadership. They were happy enough that Jack Rooney seemed to be in favor of fair pay and decent working conditions, and they liked his ideas about competing and even winning, even if those did seem rather far-fetched. But as far as this culture of his was concerned, with its moralistic talk of intangible values and behaviors, it was too new, too different, too difficult for most people to embrace voluntarily. Their position was that if Jack was so sure he had a better idea, then he (and his Ameritech imports) would first have to prove that it was more than just another flavor of the month.

For the first few years of the D.O.'s existence at U.S. Cellular—even after it had started to win converts and make a positive impact on the company—it was Jack's baby, and no one else's. It was "this Jack Rooney stuff," for better or worse, introduced by directive and enforced by fear. Even some of its early supporters were concerned that Rooney was driving the company too hard, too fast, and that they were "losing the best of U.S. Cellular" as a result. For most of the organization during these first years, the D.O. was a task imposed by the new regime. Even when it seemed to be having a beneficial effect, it was an "extra," representing an additional "to do" list beyond normal job responsibilities. "Customer focus," said one typical store manager in a 2001 focus group, "is something you do on top of your regular job."

During this time of intense change, when every system and process was under scrutiny and most jobs felt like "drinking from a fire hose," few were looking to add any of these nebulous non-essentials, like "encouraging open, two-way communication" or "listening to associate concerns and ideas" or clarifying and explaining and recognizing and coaching and providing feedback and all the rest of the D.O. line-up. Just how do you lead by inspiration anyway? And unlike conventional tasks, these D.O.-related items were never-ending. There was no box beside them to tick off when they were finished, no sense of completion or accomplishment that would allow a leader to turn the page and move on to something new. The list of responsibilities was always there, nagging like a bad conscience. "We're having trouble," admitted a leader in a written comment, "with the idea that the D.O. is never done. We're used to having a short-term goal, achieving it, and then we're done. But with the D.O., it's never done."

So the introduction of the Dynamic Organization to U.S. Cellular was very much an "outside-in" process at first, one that required the company to adopt an externally-imposed set of rules that it had to learn by rote. Most people were unable even to identify the five Values for several years, until 2003, when, to avoid another round of embarrassing revelations on the Culture Survey, some creative soul devised the acronym CREEP to ride mental herd on customer focus-respect-ethics-empowerment-pride. That worked well enough, although it still left the bigger problem of the notoriously elusive ten Behaviors.

There were a few signs during this period that some associates were beginning to internalize these new rules. They could see the difference the D.O. was making to the company, and to the way they felt about their jobs. As U.S. Cellular picked up momentum, some of the initial defensiveness began to fall away. Once they opened themselves up to the changing culture's possibilities, more and more of them were able to turn those externally-imposed rules into new habits and convictions. "We're growing, and so am I," observed a 2001 focus group participant. A colleague echoed that she had never seen a company "that offered so much challenge and gave me so much opportunity to learn."

A year later, another survey participant picked up this theme of learning and personal growth that had emerged so unexpectedly at U.S. Cellular: "The D.O. is better than any leadership book I can read. This is living, breathing inspiration, first-hand learning." Rooney still owned the culture, but more and more of his associates were claiming their share of the title. As their understanding of the D.O. increased, they began to internalize its precepts. For this growing cadre, the company and its senior leaders no longer seemed like a distant "they." More and more focus group participants referred unself-consciously to "we" when they talked about U.S. Cellular and its accomplishments.

Beginning in about 2003, the era of outside-in ended, replaced by a new period of internal study and learning and understanding and growth. The D.O. was no longer an alien philosophy imposed from beyond. It was recognized by most people as something that belonged uniquely to U.S. Cellular, even if it was not yet perfectly understood or universally owned. It was, they realized, here to stay. Rooney was obviously not going anywhere, and besides that, most of his ideas were working, giving the company and its associates "confidence and courage we never had before." The challenge, then, was to come to terms with the culture once and for all, to truly grasp and embrace it, rather than to subvert it or avoid it or get rid of it. If the D.O. was a given, the onus of change would have to transfer to individual leaders and associates.

This period of introspection and learning—roughly from 2002 to 2006—was a long phase of transition from a culture driven from outside and above to one that emanates from within the individual members of the organization. It was marked by the remarkable growth in appreciation of the company and its purpose that culminated in the gratifying survey results of 2004 and 2005. During these years, the survey recorded thousands of positive comments about nearly everything connected with U.S. Cellular: its intense customer focus, its senior leadership, the high and unbending ethical standards, the steadfast pursuit of its vision, the caring and respect for each associate, the courage to march to its own drum. These comments were overwhelmingly about the company and the rewarding jobs it provided its associates. They were not, for the most part, about the participants themselves and their own growth as individuals. That would come later. For now, they were simply developing a remarkable appreciation—"love" is not too strong a word, entering U.S. Cellular's vocabulary in 2005 when more than 500 associate comments used it to express their feelings—for their employer and the culture it was working so hard to foster.

Typical of this outpouring was this 2004 comment, one of several hundred that year on the same theme: "I've never had a job like this in my life, where I actually look forward to coming to work." That year, an engineer wrote about the "aha" moment that came to a group of U.S. Cellular associates who were taking a leadership course at a local college. The professor, at one session, asked the class when was the last time their boss had praised their work. "The U.S. Cellular people were the only ones who could answer 'today,' or 'last week.' Nobody else said anything. Until after the class, when they all asked if we were hiring."

Experiences like these provided external confirmation that something special had happened to their company. While these were always welcome, they were unnecessary for most associates, who by now knew perfectly well what a good thing they had going. A store manager reported in 2004 that his work was "so much fun that I take it home with me. My family says, 'Shut up, already, we know you love your job.'"

That same feeling was most flamboyantly displayed by the customer service rep in one of the call centers, whose typed comment that same year consisted of 105 repetitions of the phrase, "I love my job." She showed that she had grasped as well the culture's essential journey-not-the-destination quality by embedding into her mash note—right after repetition #70—her opinion that "something should be done about the scheduling process, it's difficult, if not impossible, to get weekends off" before rolling on through the last 35 choruses.

It was during this long learning phase that the first evidence began to emerge that the organization was doing more than just earning its associates' admiration. In some cases, in limited numbers at first and increasingly each year, the company was actually having a positive influence on its own people. It was not just one of those very rare instances of a culture change initiative actually changing a company. In this case, the changed company was also changing for the better some of the associates who worked there.

By 2004, survey participants were writing with genuine excitement about what they were discovering. "You can see the D.O. in our actions. It's about what you are when nobody's looking," was the opinion of a sales associate. A director from network operations wrote, "This organization has changed me. It has shown me what true leadership is all about." A year later, that process had accelerated: "There's been a growth in our knowledge of what's been in front of us for five years. You realize that the Values provide answers to everything we face every day." The process of internalizing the culture was summarized by another writer this way: "It's the way we breathe as a company." As individuals learned to share that breathing rhythm, the culture became part of them. "It's how we live. It goes home with me. I now expect the D.O. everywhere. My five-year-old says, 'That's not dynamic!'"

This theme of personal transformation as a byproduct of the D.O. was becoming a powerful sub-text of the Culture Survey

results. In some cases, this was an effect of the formal training that supported the culture. A regional engineering leader
was proud of the fact that "we're asking front-line engineers to
improve their people skills. They pooh-poohed it at first. Now
they're telling us that it's helping them at home." To a sales
manager, it was "awesome" that any company would "spend
so much time and money and effort developing character."

More often, however, the process was more like osmosis:
"The culture of this company is so positive that I find my attitude is always positive too, even in my personal life." A sales
rep was among the many who were beginning to feel that
"working at U.S. Cellular has changed my life." A peer went
further: "This company is different. Working here is almost
like being retrained for life."

INSIDE-OUT: TAKING IT TO THE STREETS

In betting its future on culture change, U.S. Cellular set out
in 2000 to win the minds and hearts of a work force that now
has doubled in size, to nearly 9,000 associates. The odds were
heavy against success, based on the unhappy past experiences of
companies a lot bigger and richer than it was. But Jack Rooney's
determination and forcefulness established an "outside-in"
beachhead, and from that point an internal momentum for
change developed that, by 2006, had brought the company
within sight of its unlikely goal.

U.S. Cellular had, by then, transformed itself according to
Rooney's model, and its associates had reached the point of
unprecedented appreciation for what it had become. The way
they talked about their company, so freely evoking feelings—

caring, pride, love—that are rarely displayed in the workplace, made it clear that the culture had penetrated deep into the emotional core of much of the organization. In changing a company, the Dynamic Organization had inevitably changed many of its individual leaders and associates as well.

The company had worked hard and purposefully to bring these changes about. Rooney's old mantra—"change people . . . or change people"—had driven much of the internal transformation, forcing many who would have preferred to avoid wrenching self-examination to confront their values and priorities, or pay the penalty. He had built a top-notch learning infrastructure dedicated to facilitating this process. No surprise, then, that after several years of single-minded pursuit of these goals, a high percentage of U.S. Cellular's population was in transit, mentally at least, examining fundamental assumptions, confronting personal demons, pores wide open to new possibilities, willing now to move into previously uncharted territory. This was an intentional and necessary outcome of the culture change process.

People, as we have noted, do not change easily. Once those minds and hearts are open and on the move, however, there is no telling where they will end up. When the results of the 2007 Culture Survey were in, it was clear that change was spreading further than anyone had realized. The things that associates had learned at work were not just affecting the internal culture, bringing individuals into alignment with the precepts of the Dynamic Organization. They were, in many cases, bubbling over into associates' other roles outside the company, as family members and citizens. In one of the most perceptive comments ever to appear on the survey, a sales rep wrote, "The D.O.'s not just 8 to 5. It's full life. Jack wanted us to take it home with us." In its moving simplicity, this is probably also one of the most memorable testimonials to a CEO we have ever seen.

Hundreds of survey participants wanted to bear witness to the positive changes they had seen in their own lives as a result of what they had learned at work. They had become, quite simply, better people. "I believe I'm becoming a better servant leader, husband, father, son, brother, and friend because I work here," wrote another 2007 participant. That theme is echoed again and again: "I now see how much U.S. Cellular has helped me grow as an individual to become not just a better associate, but a better friend, mom, and wife. For that, I could never thank it enough." A new call center service rep came to his first coach with tears in his eyes. "I'm thirty years old, and I've never made my mother proud before," he said, "but in this company, I can." A store manager described his experience in a written comment: "The leadership journey we took here over the past year and a half changed my life, both personally and professionally. I am a better person for working here."

Others described their personal moment of truth: "It's a very humbling experience when things 'click' and you realize you have to change. You have to face the things you struggled with your whole life, all your imperfections." Another associate agreed that as the Values "become part of your whole life, you clarify who you want to associate with and what you don't want to settle for."

This is remarkable stuff, springing up from deep inside an associate population that, like most of the wireless industry, is overwhelmingly young and not very rich in life experience.

Many of these people represent the alphabet soup of recent generations—X, Y, Millennial—whose common denominator seems to be that they are neither as serious nor as engaged as their predecessors, representing unlikely raw material for the culture-minded employer. They joined U.S. Cellular looking for a job in wireless or retail, often after bouncing through several other companies, usually just as young and callow and self-absorbed as any other twenty- or thirty-something. Then they encountered Jack Rooney (old enough to be a grandfather to many of them) and his core conviction that people of any age crave a sense of purpose beyond themselves, that they need to feel proud of their contributions, that they long to be treated as if they mattered—and got hooked, their whole lives changing in the process.

"It is not unprofessional to be excited."

—JACK ROONEY

Many of these converts dug deep to find the words to describe the experience. "I feel a strong internal drive to work hard within this company," said one of them. "I do not know where my career path will take me, but the values and beliefs of this company inspire me at work and in my personal life every day." Another offered that "I have grown both professionally and personally. I will carry the D.O. with me wherever I may go (but, hopefully, not outside the company). I never want to leave."

None of these people write for a living, but many of them achieved real eloquence. "I have been here for a year now, and as U.S. Cellular has changed, so have I. The leaders I am privileged to work with have inspired me to change my thinking, both at work and in my life."

When Myra Kruger read out this comment at the beginning of the 2007 Leadership Forum, the exuberant crowd was silenced by its depth of feeling: "I came here looking for a job to help pay the bills, never believing this company was really any different than any other. I couldn't have been more wrong! I have consistently felt appreciated, supported, loved, challenged, and motivated. This has not just affected the way I've felt about work, but about my own character."

The writer, a call center coach, goes on to describe the simple alchemy through which this miracle occurred. "I did not believe that there was a company that would promote individuals to positions of leadership that truly cared about others. From my first day of training, my center director has known my name and used it every time she sees me. Managers remember my husband's and child's names. I know they see the good in me first, above all else, and if they see something that isn't as good as it could be, they will address it so that I can become more than I ever dreamed I could be, and begin to grow into the person they seem to have always known I could be. Sometimes, in my regular life, I don't feel like I am all that important, but when I come to work, I always know I am."

And then she concludes: "Please tell Jack, 'Thank you.'"

What company, seven years in the shadow of Enron, can evince tributes like this: "This model is how we want to live our lives." Or this: "This company, and what it is trying to accomplish, is my role model." These, remember, are unsolicited comments, offered freely on the blank back page of a survey or in the context of a group interview where the focus is on problems and opportunities for improvement. The frequency of such sentiments, and the evident emotion involved in bringing them to the surface, stunned us as we were privileged to read and hear them.

Many associates, wakened to new possibilities by U.S. Cellular, wondered why the rest of the world can't work this way: "I wish we could infect the rest of the nation with the D.O.," was one customer service rep's interesting approach to the subject. A store manager was equally ardent, if more traditional in his choice of words: "We're the model, the shining beacon." "This company," summarized a once-skeptical director who has grown and matured into a wonderful leader, "has become extremely significant."

The message conveyed so powerfully in these comments is that the Dynamic Organization is out of control. It has moved well beyond Rooney's original ambition of animating an internal culture strong enough to drive his business model. That ambition, at one time, seemed unlikely enough, given the lack of precedent. But by now—late 2008—the long outside-in action of that culture-building process is essentially complete, a true "mission accomplished" except for the ongoing challenges of bringing new recruits seamlessly into the fold and "defending the D.O." against careless erosion.

What he could not have predicted is what happened when the spirit of the Dynamic Organization burrowed as deeply into the inner life of his associates as it has. Once their hearts were in play, there was no slowing the momentum. These people, having experienced the liberating power of the Dynamic Organization at work, carried their new perspective beyond U.S. Cellular and its customers, to all their relationships.

The trajectory of the D.O. is now inside-out, rebounding from the inner recesses of the company and its people to the larger community and the multitudes for whom U.S. Cellular remains a "best-kept secret." Rooney has finally consented, in Project Mythos, to harness this outward-bound energy, so that the brand—Believe in Something Better—becomes a mirror of the culture, matching external image with internal reality. In fact, he had no choice. The culture had become too powerful an influence to contain within the organization. Whether the company—and the world—is ready or not, the people of U.S. Cellular, knowing in their hearts that there is something better, are taking their culture to the streets.

EPILOGUE:
THE LEGACY

In some ways, U.S. Cellular's future is as uncertain as it was in the spring of 2000, when it took a flier on Jack Rooney and his bold notion of a Dynamic Organization. Nine years later, it is taking an even bigger gamble, staking its reputation and everything it has achieved on Project Mythos and the belief that consumers will want to connect with a company that puts them first; that means what it says; that seeks to be judged on the quality of the experience it provides. It may be the first company in history to invite its customers, through their experiences with its associates, to define its brand.

U.S. Cellular faces other uncertainties that could affect its future as much as Project Mythos. Rooney is approaching retirement at some as-yet-unspecified moment in the next few years. Who will his successor be, and how will the new CEO feel about the Dynamic Organization? Will the heir be an insider, with a view to providing maximum continuity? Or will the replacement come from outside, with new ideas and an urge to make a personal mark? It seems hard to imagine dismantling a culture as painstakingly built, as beloved by the organization, as good for the business as this has been—but stranger things have happened.

Another danger is less overt but just as serious: the threat from within. Twice in the past two years large parts of the company have become complacent or distracted and let core elements of the Dynamic Organization deteriorate dangerously before catching themselves and recovering their balance. Some leaders seem prone to forgetting the qualities that have allowed the company to thrive; a few may never have really believed in them at all, deep in their heart of hearts. Rooney has always been there to watch for the missteps and hurl his passion into the breach, but what happens when that safety net is no longer there?

Who knows what will happen? The current uncertain state of the U.S. economy will certainly have something to say about the outcome, as will the equally unpredictable political process. In a year or two, U.S. Cellular and the Dynamic Organization could be a success story for the ages, a phenomenon to be studied for generations—or it could be just a worthy footnote, one of the nobler chapters in the long history of corporate culture change.

Whatever happens next, however, will not diminish what this company has accomplished in these wonderful years. U.S. Cellular has grown from one of the industry's marginal bit-players and niche-fillers to a tough, respected competitor that is almost impossible to dislodge from its chosen markets. It has twice as many associates as it had in 2000, and three times as many customers. Both groups stay for the long haul. "America's most loyal customers" are served by equally steadfast associates. The appalling voluntary turnover rate of 2000 is now barely 12 percent.

The culture itself is more solidly entrenched than ever. The 2008 Culture Survey results were even better than in 2007, across the board. Those numbers have reached levels that are so far beyond ordinary standards that they might seem meaningless (just as the term "a trillion dollars" used to be), if it were not for the extraordinarily compelling witness to personal and group transformation that supports them. When the first shockwaves of the recession began to hit the company in the fall of 2008, there was no panic at U.S. Cellular. Rooney could simply remind his forces, as he did in a remarkable letter, to "take care of our customers" as they struggled to weather the economic storm, confident that the shared values necessary to carry that message into the marketplace were built on bedrock.

The remarkable events of the first quarter of 2009 demonstrated once again how well Rooney knows his people. As the economy continued to deteriorate, shedding jobs in frightening numbers, U.S. Cellular kept its focus and took care of business. Its re-branding picked up momentum around the new mantra of "Human Coverage." Sales results held up, actually increasing over the same period of the prior year. And then – right at the point where the daily drumbeat of disturbing economic news threatened the equilibrium of even the true believers – Rooney presented his company with what may be another game-changer.

He outlined his plans in a four-page message to every associate. "We intend," he said, "to protect this company and everything we have built here" by turning the recession into "an opportunity to build a better, stronger company."

Appealing to the organization's fighting heart, he assumed a characteristically aggressive stance: "We intend to do more than just survive – we expect to grow, this year and every year, and we intend to emerge from this recession more prepared to thrive than ever before."

This was more than bluster. He backed his words with a company commitment to make a major investment in six major projects that would at long last address the weak links in the company's infrastructure.

Just as important, this investment would not come at the expense of jobs and lives. Cost containment would be an element of the strategy, but the company would not look for savings from the front line associates that are its heart and soul (or even from the many front line leaders who had written to Rooney offering to sacrifice their own pay if the company needed it to protect associates' jobs).

When it did reorganize a few months later, only a few jobs were affected; even fewer associates left the company, and only after they had been given a chance to find other positions internally. After the dust cleared, an outpouring of appreciation and renewed commitment rolled through the organization. One young sales leader's reaction to these events spoke for an entire company: "I am humbled and honored to work at such a great place in these times." U.S. Cellular stayed true to its values in the face of crisis; it will continue to compete and fight and thrive; it has given its people the chance to write more chapters in its story.

U.S. Cellular has successfully defied the conventional

wisdom that only the big national players can win, and that consolidation must inevitably crush the regional outliers. It has not only survived and prospered; it has helped shape the way its competitors approach the marketplace.

The company is a proven winner among all its constituencies by every measurable standard: customer appreciation, associate satisfaction, share price, bottom line. Its walls are lined with the tangible evidence of this success: the "best wireless service" plaques and the customer loyalty trophies and the community service honors and the "best place to work" awards.

Underlying this record is the most remarkable, and perhaps the most long-lasting, achievement of them all. Jack Rooney and his slowly-expanding team of believers challenged the long-prevailing assumptions that business is a blood sport, that the advantage inevitably goes to the ruthless and the greedy, that the only way to win is to hold your nose and leave your values at the door. He has proved beyond question, once and for all, regardless of what happens from here on, that a values-based model works, that it can raise both a company and the individuals who are part of it to undreamed-of heights, to peak experiences that will last a lifetime and change the way those lives are lived. He has shown that there is indeed a better way.

This is Jack Rooney's legacy to all of us.